DEDICATION

W0028080

Insert dedication text here. Insert dedication text here. Insert dedication text here. Insert dedication text here. Insert dedication text here. Insert dedication text here. Insert dedication text here. Insert dedication text here. Insert dedication text here. Insert dedication text here. Insert dedication text here.

CONTENTS

Table of Contents

ACKNOWLEDGMENTS

Thanks to my family for being patient during the long hours invested in writing this book and putting up with my experiments as I tested various methods of water purification. Without their support, this book would not exist.

Also, I want to thank Mother Nature for throwing enough hurricanes, ice storms and blizzards my way over my life to hammer home the huge value of being prepared.

1 INTRODUCTION

Water is critical for survival. If you do not have water, you can die in as little as three days and even before then, the effects of dehydration can make you less effective and even delirious.

It is even more critical than food as we can live for several weeks without food. It is not a comfortable feeling but it is a simple fact that food is not as critical to immediate survival as is food.

Yet most people are woefully unprepared for even a very short term disaster. You see evidence of this in the news when you see supermarket shelves completely wiped out when a hurricane or significant winter storm is bearing down on an area. The bread and water aisles look like some sort of ghost town as all the folks who live the core essence of sustainable living literally one day at a time.

And if a situation lasts for more than a few days, you see all the news reports of the government not doing enough to get emergency supplies to all these woefully unprepared people. You see the FEMA vans passing out cases of water and MREs to long lines of tired, irritated and often unappreaciative people.

Don't let yourself be one of these people.

Be one of the families who ride out the event in the comfort of your home, living on supplies you laid out well before any disaster was even on the horizon.

A little advance planning can make you secure for quite a long time – long enough for things to get reasonably back to normal and supply lines to again function with some degree of efficiency.

Each chapter of this book will educate you on one aspect of water safety and security. Here is what you will find in each chapter.

Chapter 2: **Disasters That Can Trigger Your Water Plan** is a frank look at the various types of disasters that can affect you and your community. It examines the type of damage you can expect and how it can affect your life during and after the event.

Chapter 3: **Negative Effects Of A Lack Of Water** is an in depth examination of the effects of dehydration on your body. It discusses the various stages of dehydration, exploring the symptoms and negative impacts you will experience at each state.

Chapter 4: **Water Toxins And Contaminants** discusses all the biological, chemical and other dangers that can contaminate water. It looks at the various agents, their symptoms and effects on your body as well as treatment options if so afflicted.

Chapter 5: **Living A Day Without Water** is an introspective look at what life would be like without the running water that we take for granted. By reading this chapter and applying it to your own situation, you will develop a deep understanding of all the ways water touches your life on a daily basis. This will help you build a water storage/replenishment plan specific to your prioritized needs.

Chapter 6: **Build A Comprehensive Water Storage Plan** will guide you towards water independence in emergencies by helping you build a roadmap you can use to build your water supplies and likely equipment you need to acquire more potable water during an emergency situation.

Chapter 7: **How To Test Your Water's Safety** examines the steps you need to take to ensure that your water is safe to drink. As demonstrated time and again, water, even municipal water, can get contaminated. You will learn how to identify signs of water contamination and what you can learn from testing.

Chapter 8: **How To Purify Water** discusses the many ways to purify water and make it potable. A smart water storage plan has two elements: water that is immediately usable and equipment that can be used to purify external sources of water that are likely to be available to you in an emergency. This chapter helps you with the latter.

Chapter 9: **Long Term Water Storage** goes over all the issues of storing water long term and how you can build a bulletproof water storage system that will serve you safely during long term disasters.

Chapter 10: **How To Acquire Water In An Emergency** will expand your mind to the possibilities of water all around you when a disaster hits. When you finish this chapter, you will know tons of sources – both in your house and in nature – that can supplement your stored water supply.

Chapter 11: W**ater Conservation And Rationing** looks at ways you can use less water. By learning to use less when times are fine, you will find it easier to make due with less if you are ever in a situation where you need to ration water – and if you are on municipal water, these methods will help you cut your water bill and save money.

Chapter 12: **Water And Sanitation** is a vital issue. In an emergency, dirty water and a dirty environment can kill you. This chapter will discuss the steps you can take to keep you and your environment safe and clean when good quality water is scarce.

Appendices: Finally, the appendices will give you several suggestions for supplies to help you build up your water storage program, give you guidance in building your master water storage plan and share many resources for additional reading on the subjects discussed in this book.

This book does not need to be read from front to back to give you benefit. Pick the chapters that are most relevant to your current needs and study them. And then as time and interest permits, read the other chapters to fill in any knowledge gaps you have about water and survival.

There is no greater gift that you can give your family than water security. The information in this book, when applied, will ensure your family will always have clean drinking water no matter what emergency you need to handle.

2 DISASTERS THAT CAN TRIGGER YOUR WATER PLAN

If you are lucky, you live your life without encountering any serious disasters. You might experience some inconveniences like having a big storm blow in and losing power for a few hours or have your roof leak during a hard rainstorm. These are very minor inconveniences and just a part of everyday life.

However, others will not be so fortunate. They will experience disasters that last for a long term - disasters that remove you from all your normal sources of food, water and other everyday supplies: the supermarket, the tap, your well, etc. These bigger disasters can keep you trapped in your home for days or weeks waiting for help to come. And you need to be prepared if you are going to ensure your family's health and well being when you get caught up in one.

These natural and man driven disasters can happen at any time and can strike anywhere. To give you an idea of the types of events that can befall you (depending on where you live), consider:

- Tornadoes

- Hurricanes

- Extended power outage

- Ice storm

- Flood

- Chemical spill

- Earthquake

- Volcanic eruption

- Forest fire

- Tsunami

- Terrorist attack

- Industrial accident

- Broken water supply line

- Etc.

As you can see, there are many events that can disrupt your life and your ability to get fresh, clean drinking water and other supplies needed for life. And you will notice that while some events are location specific (like hurricanes and volcanoes), others can occur anywhere. For instance, an industrial accident or large fire can occur in any region. Even something as simple as a significant break in a water line can contaminate your drinking water source for days.

Let's examine some of these disaster scenarios in more detail. We will look at what they are and how they can cause a disruption of your normal water supply.

Tornadoes

A tornado is a narrow, violently rotating column of air (a funnel) that extends from the base of a thunderstorm to the ground. Tornadoes are the most violent of all atmospheric storms.

Tornadoes occur in many parts of the world, including the United States, Australia, Europe, Africa, Asia, and South America. Even New Zealand reports about 20 tornadoes each year. Two of the highest concentrations of tornadoes outside the U.S. are Argentina and Bangladesh.

In the United States, approximately 1,200 tornadoes touch down every year. They can last from several seconds to more than an hour. Most tornadoes last less than 10 minutes.

Most of the damage from a tornado happens in one of two direct ways:

1. exposure to extreme wind

2. impact by flying debris.

In a developed area, a tornado essentially acts as a giant

blender full of millions of small and large projectiles - boards, broken glass, nails, shingles, gravel, wire, cables, sheet metal, hardware, tree parts, whole trees, rocks, bricks, appliances, furniture, household items, even vehicles and large parts of houses. Basically anything the funnel can pick up gets mixed up in it and spewed out at high speed at anything in the debris path.

And all the damage is not limited to the actual event. Often a tornado will weaken a building enough that parts or all of it collapses well after the event is over due to structural weakness and imbalances. This is why people should not enter a heavily damaged home or other building until fire officials and an engineer can survey it and deep it safe for reentry.

Another danger is that hazardous materials may have been released by the tornado - such as natural gas, medical waste, gasoline, other dangerous chemicals, or sewage. A tornado does not differentiate in what it picks up and spreads around. Such "HAZMAT" releases, along with live electrical wires, also can be a cause of indirect tornado damage - either chemically or through fires. Broken water pipes can cause considerable water and flood damage also.

Combining this mix of hazardous substances with broken water pipes or contamination of an above ground water supply is a recipe for disaster. With all the other damage caused by the tornado, it could be days before your water is restored and it is very likely that boil water alerts will be in effect for an extended period of time.

Just to give you an idea how destructive a tornado can be, look at this example that hit a fairly densely populated area in Oklahoma. On May 3, 1999 parts of Oklahoma City – a major population center - were hit by a tornado.

Because of excellent, timely watches and warnings and intense media coverage of the Oklahoma tornado long before it hit, only 36 people were killed. However, the damage toll to structures and cleanup exceeded $1 billion. If there wasn't good media coverage or if the path of the tornado shifted just a bit, the damage and loss of life would have been much greater.

In the aftermath Bill Clinton declared it a disaster area and had FEMA come in to help the people who lost their homes and to allow disaster relief money to flow into the region. Even with this quick action, debris removal did not begin until May 12 and it took months to rebuild the devastated area. We are fortunate in the United States to have good support infrastructure for emergencies but they do take time to mobilize and start offering assistance. If you weren't prepared and were in the middle of such a disaster zone, life could be very difficult for a while.

Hurricanes

A hurricane is a type of storm called a tropical cyclone. I typically forms over warm tropical or subtropical waters. When a storm's maximum sustained winds reach 74 mph, it is called a hurricane and the wind speed determines the strength of the hurricane.

A hurricane's strength is rated by the Saffir-Simpson

Hurricane Wind Scale. It is given a rating from 1 to 5 based on a hurricane's maximum sustained winds and it can change as the storm evolves. The higher the number, the greater the hurricane's potential for property damage. Here are the categories and the wind strengths they represent.

- Category 1: Winds 119-153 km/hr (74-95 mph)

- Category 2: Winds 154-177 km/hr (96-110 mph)

- Category 3: Winds 178-208 km/hr (111-129 mph)

- Category 4: Winds 209-251 km/hr (130-156 mph)

- Category 5: Winds more than 252 km/hr (157 mph)

Hurricanes originate in the Atlantic basin, which includes the Atlantic Ocean, Caribbean Sea, and Gulf of Mexico, the eastern North Pacific Ocean, and, less frequently, the central North Pacific Ocean. Hurricane Season begins on June 1 and ends on November 30, although hurricanes can, and have, occurred outside of this time frame.

Hurricanes are hugely powerful and can cause massive amounts of damage over large areas. The strong, sustained winds and drenching downpours can cause flooding (both from rain and from the wind causing unusual high tides), destruction of property, loss of power and life. Even if you are not directly affected by a hurricane, it could stir up the local water supply or disrupt its power source, causing a boil water alert - which doesn't help if you do not have power to boil the water. Also, the flooding can cover the earth with contaminated water –

causing your well to become contaminated. If the flood waters sit long enough, your well can get contaminated with sewage and can be a source of several dangerous diseases in your well water supply. It is always a good idea to test your well water any time flooding covers the well cover as it represents a risk of contamination of that water supply.

To give you an idea of the destructive power of hurricanes, take a look at the details of hurricane Andrew.

Hurricane Andrew hit South Florida in August 1992 and at that time, it was rated the most destructive hurricane in United States history. It made landfall as a Category 5 hurricane with wind speeds up to 177 mph.

It passed directly through Homestead, Florida, a suburb south of Miami, It totally destroyed entire blocks of homes, in many cases right down to the concrete foundations. Over 25,000 houses were destroyed in Miami-Dade County from Andrew, and nearly 100,000 more were severely damaged. The damage exceeded $26 billion (1992 USD), and 65 people lost their lives in the hurricane. The only reason the loss of lives was so low is that many people evacuated before the storm made landfall.

At the time Andrew hit, I lived 60 miles north of Homestead in Fort Lauderdale. Even that far away, we were affected by Andrew. The strong winds damaged many properties and caused several power outages in the region.

The only good thing about a hurricane is you almost always know one may be coming several days before it hits. This gives you plenty of time to prepare or evacuate. Most hurricane prone cities offer shelters for people to go to when a storm comes – and they will call for mandatory evacuations of the most likely coastal impact areas to telegraph the seriousness of the storms and to do their best to minimize loss of life.

Smart people in these areas will make sure they are stocked up on food and water well before any storm is on the horizon. With a few week stockpile of food and water, you can survive at home - if it is undamaged – until either help arrives or things normalize enough for local commerce to again be operational.

Floods

Flooding is an overflowing of water onto land that is typically dry. Floods have many causes: heavy rains, ocean waves, snow melt and when dams or levees break. Flooding can be just a few inches of water or walls of water higher than your house. They can occur quickly or over a long period of time, possibly lasting weeks, or longer. Floods are the most common of all weather-related natural disasters.

Flash floods are the most dangerous kind of floods, combining the raw destructive power of a flood with speed and unpredictability. They often happen with little or no warning.

Flooding is a worldwide experience, occurring anywhere in

the world that receives rain. In the U.S. floods kill more people each year than tornadoes, hurricanes or lightning.

Floods cause such a wide array of problems that the attacks on your normal water supply are many.

Flood waters can destroy houses and erode land causing sewage to leak from septic tanks and sewer systems as they flood and spit out their contents into the flood waters. They can cause your well to become contaminated by having contaminated, standing water sitting over your well cover for days – allowing the contaminants to penetrate to the water table. Water pipes and surface aquifers can become contaminated. And of course, standing water for days on end can cause contamination of the ground as it dries and all sorts of nasty diseases – as well as blooms of nasty insects like mosquitoes.

Just to give an example of how extreme and unpredictable flooding can be, I'm writing this in October 2015, just after the 20+ inch rains hit parts of South Carolina, causing massive flash flooding and general flooding. In today's paper, the headline reads "...leaves 40,000 without drinkable water...".

Now South Carolina is not an area prone to such massive and widespread flooding so I can guarantee that most of those people are hurting right now because they didn't prepare for an event of this type – or prepare at all for that matter. This was a truly historic event, not an every year possibility like hurricane and tornado prone areas where many people prep for short term emergencies at the start of the season. And that is part of the problem. People think it won't ever happen to them so they don't make any preparations.

But it is because of events like these that prepping – at least for a short term event lasting a few weeks – is a really smart insurance policy everyone should practice no matter where they live.

As a follow up on the flod, the paper also said that a dam on Rockyford Lake burst on Monday – the day after the rain stopped. This shows that just because the rain stopped, the danger posed by flooding has not ended. It can cause damage for several days after the rain stops.

Earthquakes

An earthquake is the noticeable shaking of the surface of the Earth, which can be be very mild or violent enough to destroy major buildings and kill thousands of people. They result from the sudden release of energy in the Earth's crust, creating seismic waves that make the earth move.

Strong earthquakes can cause tremendous damage – including cracking and collapse of land which can break water, gas and sewer pipes as well as collapse buildings. It can also trigger a tsunami which will cause great flooding, fires and other secondary disasters.

Earthquakes also make it very difficult for help to get to you quickly in a severely damaged and unstable region. This means you can be stuck where you are with no running water and unknown hazards all around you. The damage can also cause sewage to enter water lines, disturb the bottom of any surface aquifers and collapse the infrastructure of any deep aquifers causing any variety of contaminants to penetrate the water supply and supply disruptions to occur.

Probably the most famous earthquake in recent history is the 2010 earthquake that hit Haiti. Even though much stronger earthquakes have hit other areas of the world recently (like in Chile recently), the one that hit Haiti was particularly destructive due to the poor infrastructure in that country.

This earthquake practically destroyed Port-au-Prince, Jacmel and other settlements in the region and killed several hundred thousand people. Needless to say, the entire water and sanitation infrastructure was destroyed and is still not completely recovered.

In addition to having no clean water supplies and no way to remove human waste, the country was beset by disease. For instance, in October, a cholera epidemic broke out, a disease that arises when there is limited access to clean water and proper sanitation.

An earthquake is potentially the most dangerous of all natural events because it can completely destroy the infrastructure – preventing help from arriving for days, weeks or longer. This means you could be stranded in your neighborhood with no way out until roads are repaired or the government can manage an airlift operation.

If you live in such an area, you should be sure your home is fortified to hopefully withstand an earthquake and you should be sure to have a large supply of food and water for emergency situations that could last weeks before help arrives.

Chemical Spill/Industrial Accident

Industry generates a huge number of waste products – many of which are dangerous contaminants if they get into our water supply. Some are deadly by themselves while others are dangerous because of secondary effects – like fertilizer running off into a lake causing a deadly algae bloom.

Some accidents are very short lived – flushing out into the ocean or naturally degrading to harmless substances. Others are not so nice. They can soak into the ground causing widespread contamination. Or they can sink into the riverbed, getting dredged up into the water supply with every hard rain, tornado, flood, hurricane, etc. literally making those types of accidents that gift that keeps on taking.

Municipal water supplies undergo frequent, rigorous testing to ensure that they do not get contaminated. But if you are using a well or other source for your water – whether for drinking or for using with your animals/irrigation for your garden, you need to be proactive about testing its quality.

It also helps if you know the history of the area – especially events that are located "upstream" from you. This will give you valuable knowledge and let you know what kind of priority you should give to your water testing frequency.

A few recent famous spills include the BP oil spill in the Gulf of Mexico that contaminated shorelines and the ocean floor and many land and ocean species. This spill potentially contaminated water sources close to shore and the quality of the Gulf food source while it was being cleaned by both man and nature.

And very recently, we have the August 2015 EPA accident at the Gold King Mine near Silverton, Colorado which included mine waste water and tailings. In this toxic slurry there were a variety of heavy metals such as cadmium and lead, and other toxic elements, such as arsenic.

It dumped millions of gallons of this sludge into the Animas River, closing it. Residents with wells in floodplains around the river were told to have their water tested before drinking it or bathing in it. They were also told to avoid contact with the river, including pets and farm animals. And they were told to not fish the river.

The long-term impacts of the spill on the nearby communities are unknown at this time.

As you can see, disasters come in many different forms and varying levels of severity. And they can literally affect anyone, anywhere.

You have an obligation to yourself and your family to prepare for these potential events. This book reaches everything you need to know to be water secure in such events. Investing in being prepared is truly the best form of insurance you can buy.

3 NEGATIVE EFFECTS OF A LACK OF WATER

Second to air, water is the most critical need for humans.

Depending on the environment, the onset of dehydration can begin in as little as one hour and can cause debilitating symptoms and even lead to death in 1-3 days depending on the general health of the person and stress the environment creates.

For instance, walking during the daytime in the middle of a hot summer desert will result in a much quicker onset of symptoms from dehydration than someone who is camped out in a shady wooded location and relaxing all day in a hammock.

Age also has a big impact on how quickly lack of water can lead to severe problems and death. Babies, the young and seniors are much more susceptible to dehydration and all its problems than adults in good health. For babies and children, it is simply based on the fact that they are small and have high metabolisms due to their growing into adulthood. And for seniors, it is a reflection of their general decline in health that comes as we all age that results in them being affected more quickly and more severely than the average healthy adult.

What is Dehydration?

Dehydration – also known as Hypohydration – is simply the state of not having enough water in the body for it to function properly. This imbalance causes a disruption of many vital metabolic processes necessary to keep you functioning at peak efficiency and eventually processes that are necessary to keep you alive.

Dehydration occurs when water intake is not sufficient to replace water lost through normal biological processes – breathing, urination, sweating – or other causes; like vomiting, diarrhea or blood loss from a wound.

While dehydration is commonly considered just a lack of water in the body, there are actually a few different types of dehydration that can impact you – all of which are related to the balance of water and salts in the body.

Hypotonic dehydration refers to a loss of electrolytes – most commonly sodium. **Hypertonic dehydration** refers to a loss of water. **Isotonic dehydration** refers to a loss of both water and electrolytes.

What this means that if you get dehydrated, just drinking water may not be sufficient to bring you back to health. This is the reason coaches make sure their athletes drink plenty of electrolyte solution during practice and competition. All the heavy exertion and sweating quickly depletes the body of both water and electrolytes.

Is dehydration something you really need to worry about?

Yes... it can affect anyone, any time. Chances are good that you have been mildly dehydrated many times in your life. An excellent example of a situation where you might induce mild dehydration is if you drive for several hours without drinking to limit the number of pit stops you need to make. While you may feel reasonably fine at the end of the trip, there is a good chance that you actually suffered mild dehydration and its symptoms for a portion of the drive.

Dehydration is a serious condition and it is not just caused by finding yourself in an emergency situation. Something as simple as a day hike in a very hot, dry climate can easily cause dehydration. Even if you are drinking water in such situations, it probably is not enough. That is why you sometimes feel poorly after spending several hours outdoors doing heavy work and why drinking a few glasses of water or electrolyte solution afterwords seems to perk you up so quickly.

What Causes Dehydration?

Now that we know what dehydration is, let's look at the many things that can bring it on.

Water can be lost from the body in "sensible" and "insensible" ways. Sensible water loss refers to water loss that you are aware of – such as sweating, urinating or vomiting. Insensible water loss is loss via mechanisms you do not notice like water loss through the skin at low levels of exertion (i.e. when you are not sweating) and through ordinary breathing.

Dehydration begins when the body goes out of homeostasis either by not taking in enough fluids or as a side effect of a disease or environmental condition that causes a water/electrolyte imbalance in your body.

Dehydration can be caused by external/stress related causes, infectious diseases, malnutrition and other causes. Let's look at several examples to give you an idea of all the ways dehydration can occur.

External/Stress Related

- Blood loss – This is pretty obvious. Blood loss is a direct loss of fluid in from your body. If you lose enough, you will be in a dehydrated state until the fluids are replaced. That is why blood donors are given orange juice and told to drink lots of water for several days after donating blood.

- Crying – Most of us leak tears from time to time. It can be from a strong wind or a strong emotional response. Most of the time, this is a very small issue but for a truly emotionally wrought person crying persistently over several hours, it can represent a significant loss of body fluids.

- Diarrhea – Diarrhea, especially in infants, is a major source of dehydration. Over the course of a day with constant bouts of diarrhea, you can lose a significant amount of body fluid – and in a baby, constant diarrhea can be deadly.

- Fever – Fevers cause you to sweat more and this additional sweating puts more demands on your body for fluid replenishment. Someone with a very high fever who is not drinking plenty of fluids can become dehydrated very quickly.

- General stress – Any stressors on your body can be exacerbated when you become dehydrated – causing a downward spiraling feedback look. Emergency situations are good examples of general stress. Your whole life is thrown into chaos and you are worrying about 10X as many things as normal and very likely have no good routine to lean back on. In these situations, you often need to remind yourself to do healthy things for yourself. It is the lack of doing these routine things – like drinking enough fluids – that sets up this dangerous feedback loop.

- Hypothermia – Hypothermia is brought about by being exposed to cold weather and having your body temperature plunge. A key mechanism to stave off the onset of hypothermia is sufficient blood volume to maintain optimal circulation in the extremities. If you are suffering dehydration, you can become hypothermic much more quickly. Therefore when operating in cold climates, it is vitally important to maintain healthy fluid intake.

- Prolonged exposure to a dry environment (5-15% humidity) or a long plane trip can accelerate the onset of dehydration. While you probably don't want to drink too much on a plane ride and have to use the bathroom multiple times, you should remember to drink extra fluids right after getting off the plane. And in a very dry environment, you want to drink more frequently than normal.

- Shock – When someone is in shock, it is important to keep them hydrated to help speed recovery. Without sufficient fluids, hypovolemic shock can set in or worsen.

- Strenuous physical activity – especially in a hot or dry environment – without taking replacement fluids

- Vomiting – Like diarrhea, constant vomiting will quickly cause dehydration and is especially dangerous for babies. If it is impossible for the person to hold fluids without vomiting, that person should seek medical help.

- Weeping burns or similar injury that results in a slow and constant loss of body fluids. It seems strange that a small loss of fluids can result in dehydration but if it is a constant slow drip, drip, drip, it can lead to a loss of fluid volume – especially in an emergency situation where getting sufficient water to replace the losses is impossible.

Infectious Diseases – Infectious diseases can bring about dehydration as they often cause vomiting or diarrhea. Common diseases that can upset your fliud balance include:

- Cholera

- Gastroenterisis

- Shigellosis

- Yellow Fever

Malnutrition – Malnutrition plays havoc with the homeostasis of the body and is often associated with dehydration. Examples of how malnutrition can affect you include:

- Electrolyte imbalance

- Fasting

- Inability to swallow

- Patient refusing food/water

- Rapid weight loss

Other causes – In addition to the above categories, there are several other things that can cause you to get dehydrated. And the common factor is we lose more fluid than we replace. If any of the below fit you, it is vital that you invest extra attention to drinking sufficient fluids as each of these situations cause your body to excrete water more rapidly.

- Acute emergency dehydration event

- Aging

- Chrohn's disease - chronic inflammatory bowel disease that affects the lining of the digestive tract.

- Dietary supplements

- Foodborne illnesses

- High altitudes

- Low carbohydrate diet

- Pregnancy

- Prescription medicines

- Severe hyperglycemia – especially in diabetics

Dehydration can also be accelerated by the consumption of diuretics which includes alcohol and caffeinated drinks.

Fortunately, dehydration is easy to stave off in most instances. The solution is simple. You simply need to drink more fluids.

Now that you have a good understanding of all the ways you can become dehydrated, let's examine the symptoms that exhibit themselves in its various stages of severity.

The Stages of Dehydration

There are three main stages of dehydration – from mild to severe. Each stage is marked by specific symptoms and outlined here.

Stage 1 Dehydration

Stage 1 dehydration is the mildest form of dehydration. It is actually a stage where we often find ourselves at various times in our lives as it takes very little to bring on this stage.

It represents a loss of about 2% of your total body fluid. Since the human body is about 75% water by weight, this represents a loss of just 2.25 pounds of weight for a person who weighs 150 pounds. You can lose this amount during a nights sleep, a vigorous exercise session or even driving for several hours without drinking water to cut down on bathroom trips. As you can see, getting to this stage of dehydration is very easy and in many ways a normal part of the cycle of life.

There are many signs your body will give you to let you know that you are mildly dehydrated and should drink some water to restore your fluid balance. They include:

- Chills

- Constipation

- Dark colored urine

- Difficulty producing saliva

- Dizziness

- Dry Mouth

- Dry skin

- Fatigue

- Lightheartedness

- Mild headache

- Reduced appetite

- Skin flushing

- Sleepiness

- Slight difficulty concentrating or focusing

- Tear production being reduced or shut down

- Thirst

At this stage, these symptoms tend to be mild and can easily be mistaken for something else. So someone in this stage of dehydration often doesn't realize that it is dehydration that is causing the problem rather than just the stress of the day or the onset of a cold.

An easy way to "tell" if you are in this stage is to drink plenty of fluids and see if you quickly start feeling better.

Stage 2 Dehydration

Stage 2 dehydration occurs when the body suffers a fluid loss equal to about 5% of your total fluid weight. In the 150 pound person example, this represents a loss of 5.6 pounds.

As you can tell, getting to this stage in a survival situation is not too difficult and demonstrates just how crucial a supply of drinking water is to your health and well being.

Stage 2 dehydration is a pretty significant condition and

has severe symptoms and consequences if not quickly treated.

Stage 2 symptoms include:

- Decreased sweating and urination

- Extreme fatigue

- Increased hear rate, temperature and respiration

- Muscle cramps

- Nausea and significant constipation

- Neurological signs- feelings of tingling and numbness

- Severe headaches

At this stage, drinking fluids can usually bring one back to health. But in some instances, it can be severe enough to require medical intervention and the application of intravenous fluids to restore balance.

Stage 3 Dehydration

Stage 3 dehydration occurs when the body suffers a fluid loss of 10% or more. This represents a fluid loss of 11.25 pounds. Stage 3 dehydration is very severe and if not treated immediately, can quickly lead to death.

Stage 3 dehydration exhibits the following symptoms:

- Chest pain

- Confusion

- Dimming of vision

- Muscle spasms

- Painful urination

- Raid pulse

- Respiratory depression

- Seizures

- Temporary blindness

- Unconsciousness

- Very low urine volume

- Vomiting

At this point, if immediate medical attention is not available to reverse the effects, this level of dehydration will quickly progress to organ damage, loss of organ function and death.

Even if you are able to supply the person with water at this stage, it generally is not enough to allow for a sufficient recovery. Generally IV fluids to restore the body's water volume and electrolyte balance are required to recover when the body has collapsed this far.

Prevention

Preventing dehydration is pretty simple − just drink enough fluids frequently enough to stay hydrated.

The amount you need to drink can vary dramatically from

day to day depending on your activity level and environmental conditions (temperature, wind, etc.) For instance, a construction worker will need to drink a lot more fluid when digging ditches all day than when enjoying a quiet weekend at home with the family.

The best way to know how much to drink is to just pay attention to what your body is saying. If you frequently notice that you are having symptoms of mild dehydration, try drinking a bit more water every day to see if they go away. If they do, you will have a pretty good indication that you were not sufficiently hydrated.

Of course, this all assumes the ready availability of water to drink.

In a survival situation, this might not be the case. There is unfortunately no good answer if you find yourself in an emergency situation with no water or other fluids to drink – but one thing you should not practice in a survival situation is saving water for later.

By not drinking enough fluids, you will definitely get dehydrated. As you saw from the symptoms above, lack of water will affect your performance and ability to deal with situations at a time when you need to be at your sharpest.

 Therefore, if water is available, you should drink your fill to restore yourself. And only then look for a way to store and carry excess for future drinking.

It has been proven time and again that rationing water in survival situations reduces your chances of surviving and getting rescued. Once stage 2 dehydration sets in, your ability to function is significantly impaired and your chances of survival drop dramatically. While it may seem counterintuitive, saving some water for the next day could be the thing that ends your life in an emergency.

When water is scarce, you want to use whatever supply is available to you to live another day. And this may mean that you need to compromise your water drinking cleanliness standards. For instance, on a hike you would probably take time to purify stream water – but in a survival situation, you may not have purification supplies available to you. In this case, drinking potentially tainted water to give you the ability to keep on moving another day could be a smart choice.

That said, **there are some fluids you should never drink** when you are suffering a water shortage as they will only serve to further dehydrate you. They include:

- Alcohol

- Blood

- Fish juices

- Melted water from new sea ice as it will be loaded with salt

- Sea water

- Urine

- Any water source that has a chemical or oil slick on it as it is most likely highly contaminated.

You should consider drinking

- Precipitation from rain, snow, dew, etc. (but melt snow before drinking)

- Surface water from streams, lakes and springs

- Ground water but only as a last resort (this is standing water with no movement in it.)

Remember, when it is a survival situation, your number one goal is getting to safety. So you may need to make decisions you would not normally make in order to get out alive. But make smart decisions – ones with the minimal likelihood to immediately impair (or poison) you.

Treatment

Treatment for dehydration depends on the level of dehydration you are experiencing.

In its most mild form, treatment is as simple as drinking water. You also need to stop fluid loss, if any. In other words, if you have an open would and are bleeding, you need to stop the bleeding. If you have a bad case of diarrhea and/or vomiting, you need to treat it so it stops. As you overcome your dehydration, you will notice that your urine concentration and frequency returns to normal. And your general feeling of wellness will improve.

For more severe dehydration, you will generally need to replace both lost fluid and restore proper electrolyte balance. Depending on the severity, this may be accomplished by drinking fluids and electrolyte drinks and keeping a careful watch on your symptoms to be sure you improve. But if you do self treat and notice no improvement, you need to get professional help – which will often involve getting IV fluids to help restore your fluid and electrolyte balance.

Are You in a High Risk Group?

While anyone can get dehydrated, certain groups are at a higher risk for dehydration than the general population.

These include:

Infants/Children – Infants and children are very vulnerable to dehydration due to their small body weight and their high turnover of electrolytes and water. They are also very likely to get diarrhea that can quickly dehydrate their small bodies.

Seniors – As people reach senior status, their bodies lose their ability to conserve water, their sense of thirst becomes less acute and they are less able to respond appropriately to temperature changes. On top of that, they often eat and drink less and certain medications and chronic diseases can multiply the impact of these issues. As a result of all these issues, seniors can reach a state of constant slight dehydration and quickly become severely dehydrated if they get sick.

People with chronic illnesses – Certain chronic illnesses can bring about dehydration. They include diabetes, kidney disease and heart failure. These issues can be compounded by colds, sore throats and fevers.

People living at high altitudes: At altitudes about 8,000 feet, dehydration chances increase due to the impact of the high altitude on your body. High altitudes can cause increased urination and more rapid breathing both of which cause you to lose water at a faster than normal rate.

People working/exercising in hot, humid weather – When you are exercising in very hot and humid weather, your ability to cool yourself via sweating is hampered. This means that your body temperature rises and if you don't counter this temperature rise with more fluids, you can get dehydrated and/or develop a heat illness.

Endurance athletes – Endurance athletes encompass the class of elite athletes who run marathons, triathlons, heavy mountain climbing, etc. These people are at a very high risk of dehydration because while exercising it is very common to lose more water than you take in. For each hour of continuous exercise, this deficit grows until it becomes a serious matter. Therefore, a good hydration regime is critical for these elite athletes.

Should You Drink Electrolyte Drinks?

Since proper electrolyte balance is vital for good health, should you constantly drink electrolyte drinks like Gatorade®?

As long as you eat a reasonably regular diet, supplementing with electrolyte drinks isn't necessary as your body does a fantastic job regulating your electrolyte balance. If you have too much, it will go out in your urine. If you have too little, your body will conserve what it has while it builds up to a proper level.

But for people who do heavy, constant manual labor or for elite athletes, electrolyte supplements can be beneficial. As long as the person is healthy and not being super excessive with electrolyte drinks, any excess will be expelled from the body in the urine.

Another class that benefits from electrolyte drinks is people with a bad case of diarrhea and/or vomiting. They are losing fluids and electrolytes at a rapid pace and an electrolyte drink can do wonders towards bringing the body back in balance.

One of the good things about electrolyte drinks is they are actually a very simple solution of water, sugar and salt. You can make your own electrolyte solution by adding 1 teaspoon of salt and eight teaspoons of sugar to a liter of water and thoroughly dissolving it before drinking. You can even add a little flavoring – like a squirt of lemon juice or some sugar free flavored drink powder.

Because making this electrolyte solution is so simple, you can make packages of the dry components to keep in your backpack, survival kit or bug out bag to use out in the field on an as needed basis. It's a lot easier to carry a few ounces of salt and sugar than carrying a few bottles of Gatorade® and it will give you as much benefit.

These sorts of little preps can make a huge difference down the line.

4 WATER TOXINS AND CONTAMINANTS

Most of us in first world economies are used to clean, safe water being no further away than the kitchen sink – or a bottle of water pulled from the refrigerator. While these water supplies do have some level of contaminants (chlorine, fluoride, etc.), they are generally considered at a low enough level to not cause harm.

And at least the chlorine or its equivalent is serving a useful purpose – killing the biological contaminants that may be found in the source water supply. This is exactly the same process you would execute on a survival water supply. The only difference is the quantity of chlorine you need to add to the water. You are dealing with drops and the municipalities are dealing with huge quantities but the end result is the same – biologically quiet water.

But once we step away from these "safe" sources of water, the rules can change quickly. The first step away is getting water from a well. It can be or become contaminated. And when we find ourselves in a survival situation where we may be drinking water from streams, ponds, lakes and even puddles, we suddenly find ourselves at a potentially high risk of ingesting dangerous impurities.

There are many different types of contaminants we can encounter in our water supply. They include:

- bacteria and viruses

- heavy metal contaminants

- Nitrates

- Poisonous chemicals

- and much more...

As a prepper, it is important to understand all these potential hazards. Once you understand them, you can learn how to avoid them or render them harmless. This knowledge (and appropriate purification equipment when appropriate) will ensure that you have a safe supply of drinking water to sustain you through any emergency you may encounter.

This chapter discusses the various contaminants you can encounter in your water sources. A future chapter discusses the many ways to purify water and how the various methods remove the many contaminants that may be in your water supply.

Biological Contaminants

The first area we will examine are living organisms. Most

"wild" water supplies will have some level of biological contaminants in them. These contaminants include protozoa, bacteria, viruses, water carried worms and algae.

People who travel to Mexico are warned not to drink the water or they may suffer from Montezuma's revenge (diarrhea) because their digestive tracts are not used to the biological contaminants in their drinking water. But to the locals, they are relatively harmless as they have adapted to the lower quality of their water supplies. So in some instances, the danger of biological agents is relative. But in other cases, they can be deadly to anyone if left untreated.

Let's examine each category of biological contaminants so you understand what they are and how they can harm you if ingested.

Protozoa

Protozoa are very small (microscopic) organisms but in terms of the size of the various organic contaminants, they are actually the largest organisms that can contaminate your water supply. Typically protozoa and their cysts range in size from 2 to 50 microns. [A micron is one millionth of a meter or 1/25,400th of an inch so it is a very small organism.]

There are many health issues that can be caused by protozoa (discussed below), the most common being from

Giardia Lamblia (aka Giardia) and Cryptosporidium (aka Crypto.)

Protozoa can cause severe sickness and death – especially in the young, old and those with a compromised immune system. But for healthy adults, they are more likely to cause diarrhea and related gastrointestinal sickness or have no impact.

Protozoa can be found in many common water supplies – even public water supplies. If you are using water from a natural spring or a well, testing for protozoa contamination is highly recommended.

The easiest way to prevent issues from protozoa in your water source is with a filtration system that uses a filter that catches all contaminants greater in size than one micron. Since protozoa are at least two microns in size, the filter will capture all of the protozoa and give you full protection from this contaminant.

Bacteria

The next smallest biological contaminant you are likely to encounter is bacteria. They are smaller than protozoa – ranging in size from 0.2 to 0.6 microns. Therefore, if you are filtering water and want to stop bacteria from passing through, you will need a filter that can catch objects as small as 0.2 microns. any larger filter size will allow bacteria to flow through it and into your drinking water.

Bacteria in water are responsible for many diseases (more below) including typhoid fever, cholera, diarrhea and dysentery. Bacterial infections can cause severe diarrhea and dehydration that can be fatal if not treated.

Viruses

Viruses are the smallest organic contaminant – ranging in size from 0.02 to 0.03 microns. Viruses are too small to be filtered out by a mechanical filter. Viruses typically contaminate water supplies that are exposed to human waste and are quite rare in clean water supplies. Like protozoa, most viruses are not deadly in a healthy adult but some can be deadly.

Algae

Algae are a simple plant that range in size from the microscopic to one hundred feet or longer in the case of some seaweeds. For our purposes, we are talking about microalgae. The most common microalgae are green, brown, red and cyanobacteria (also known as blue-green algae.)

Algae are generally harmless and provide many benefits to the ecosystem – serving as food for a variety of animals. But under the right conditions, an algae bloom can happen and literally choke the ecosystem causing widespread death of the creatures living in that ecosystem – which by itself creates unhealthy water.

But there can be other issues. Some species of cyanobacteria produce toxins during these blooms. These toxins can cause harm to people, wildlife, and pets when they drink the contaminated water. There is also some evidence that these toxins can accumulate in freshwater fish and shellfish meaning that there can be a long term negative impact to those who eat seafood from previously contaminated water sources.

Worms, Parasites and Fungi

The last class of biological contaminant is fungi, worms and parasites. The list of these parasitic organisms include ringworm, hookworm, lice and many other water based organisms.

There are literally hundreds of potential biological contaminants that can make you sick or even cause death. Most are found in very poor countries where basic sanitation and water treatment are nonexistent. But they can show up in any area where access to clean sanitation is restricted for a long period of time – like in severe flood situations where water mixes with sewage and takes days or weeks to subside.

Depending on your water source, you can encounter different groups of biological contaminants. The CDC (Centers for Disease Control and Prevention) made a few nice lists that are reproduced below to help you understand what the most likely contaminants are for your day to day water source. The lists include both biological contaminants and other types of contaminants (discussed later in this chapter.)

The most common contaminants in public (municipal) water systems include:

- Giardia

- Legionella

- Norovirus

- Shigella

- Campylobacter

- Copper

- Salmonella

- Cryptosporidium

- E. coli

- Excess fluoride

- Hepatitis A

In wells, the most common contaminants include:

- Arsenic

- Copper

- Cryptosporidium

- Campylobacter

- E. coli

- Enterovirus

- Giardia

- Hepatitis A

- Lead

- Nitrate

- Norovirus

- Radon

- Rotavirus

- Salmonella

- Shigella

In other water supplies (streams, ponds, lakes, etc.), you can be exposed to any of the contaminants in the above two lists.

Now that we understand the basic classes of biological contaminants, lets examine list of the more common waterborne biological contaminants in detail. We will explore how they can affect you, the typical symptoms you may experience and recommended treatment options.

Campylobacter

Campylobacter bacteria causes an infectious disease called Campylobacteriosis. It is a very common disease, estimated to affect over 1.3 million people in the United States every year.

Most cases of campylobacteriosis are associated with eating raw or undercooked poultry or from cross-contamination of other foods by these items – usually from cooks working with chicken and then uncooked foods like salad without washing their hands and work surface in between. Large outbreaks of Campylobacter have most often been associated with unpasteurized dairy products, contaminated water, poultry, and produce.

Most people who become ill with campylobacteriosis get:

- diarrhea

- cramping

- abdominal pain

- fatigue

- and fever

within two to five days after exposure to the organism. The diarrhea may be bloody and can be accompanied by nausea and vomiting. The illness typically lasts about one week. Some infected people do not have any symptoms. In people with compromised immune systems, Campylobacter occasionally spreads to the bloodstream and causes a serious life-threatening infection. While it can cause death, it is quite rare. The CDC estimates that approximately 70 people die from this disease every year.

Almost all persons infected with Campylobacter recover without any specific treatment. Patients should drink extra fluids as long as the diarrhea lasts to prevent dehydration. Antimicrobial therapy is warranted only for patients with severe disease or those at high risk for severe disease, such as those with immune systems severely weakened from medications or other illnesses. Azithromycin and fluoroquinolones (e.g., ciprofloxacin) are commonly used for treatment of these infections, but resistance to fluoroquinolones is common. In fact resistance to antimicrobials is rising, and the CDC has designated drug-resistant Campylobacter a serious public health threat.

Prevention is fairly simple. Simple food handling and cleanliness practices can help prevent Campylobacter infection.

- Wash hands before preparing food

- Wash hands immediately after handling raw poultry or other meat

- Wash thoroughly with soap and hot water all food preparation surfaces and utensils that have come in contact with raw meat

- Cook poultry products thoroughly

- Don't drink unpasteurized milk

- Don't drink unchlorinated water that isn't boiled

- Wash hands after handling pet feces or visiting petting zoos

Cholera

Cholera is an acute, diarrheal illness caused by infection of the intestine with the bacterium Vibrio cholerae and is spread by ingestion of contaminated food or water. The infection is often mild or without symptoms, but sometimes it can be severe and life threatening. According to the World Health Organization, an estimated 3-5 million cases and over 100,000 deaths occur each year around the world.

A person can get cholera by drinking water or eating food contaminated with the cholera bacterium. Large epidemics are often related to fecal contamination of water supplies or street vended foods. The disease is occasionally spread through eating raw or undercooked shellfish that are naturally contaminated.

Approximately one in ten (5-10%) of infected persons will have severe cholera which in the early stages includes:

- profuse watery diarrhea

- vomiting

- rapid heart rate

- loss of skin elasticity

- dry mucous membranes

- low blood pressure

- thirst

- muscle cramps

- and restlessness or irritability.

Persons with severe cholera can develop acute renal

failure, severe electrolyte imbalances and coma. If untreated, severe dehydration can rapidly lead to shock and death in hours.

Assuming that the illness is severe enough to need treatment, there are three treatment regimens that are followed:

- Rehydration therapy, delivering a prompt restoration of lost fluids and salts through proper rehydration methods. This is typically delivered via oral rehydration salts and, when necessary, intravenous fluids and electrolytes.

- Antibiotic treatment, which reduces fluid requirements and duration of illness, is indicated for severe cases of cholera.

- Zinc treatment via zinc supplementation has been shown to help improve cholera symptoms in children.

Crypto(sporidium)

Cryptosporidium is a microscopic parasite that causes the diarrheal disease cryptosporidiosis. Both the parasite and the disease are commonly known as "Crypto."

There are many species of Cryptosporidium that infect animals, some of which also infect humans. The parasite is protected by an outer shell that allows it to survive outside the body for long periods of time and makes it very tolerant to chlorine disinfection. However, using a filter that filters out contaminants larger than 1 micron will remove all instances of Cryptosporidium from your water supply.

While this parasite can be spread in several different ways, water (drinking water and recreational water) is the most common way to spread the parasite. Cryptosporidium is a leading cause of waterborne disease among humans in the United States.

Symptoms of cryptosporidiosis generally begin 2 to 10 days (average 7 days) after becoming infected with the parasite. The most common symptom of cryptosporidiosis is watery diarrhea. Symptoms include:

- Watery diarrhea

- Stomach cramps or pain

- Dehydration

- Nausea

- Vomiting

- Fever

- Weight loss

Some people with Crypto will have no symptoms at all. For those with symptoms, they will usually last about 1 to 2 weeks (with a range of a few days to 4 or more weeks) in persons with healthy immune systems. Occasionally, people may experience a recurrence of symptoms after a brief period of recovery before the illness ends. Symptoms can come and go for up to 30 days.

Most people who have healthy immune systems will recover without treatment. Diarrhea can be managed by drinking plenty of fluids to prevent dehydration. People who are in poor health or who have weakened immune systems are at higher risk for more severe and prolonged illness.

Young children and pregnant women may be more susceptible to dehydration resulting from diarrhea and should drink plenty of fluids while ill. Rapid loss of fluids from diarrhea may be especially life threatening to babies. Therefore, parents should talk to their healthcare providers about fluid replacement therapy options for infants if they have become infected.

Dysentery

Dysentery is an inflammation of the intestine causing diarrhea with blood. Other symptoms may include fever, abdominal pain, and rectal tenesmus (a feeling of incomplete defecation).

Dysentery is caused by a number of types of infection such as bacteria, viruses, parasitic worms, or protozoa (aka amoebic dysentery). The mechanism if infection is an inflammatory disorder of the intestine, especially of the colon.

Dysentery is managed by maintaining fluids by using oral rehydration therapy. If this treatment cannot be adequately maintained due to vomiting or the profuseness of diarrhea, hospital admission may be required for intravenous fluid replacement.

E. Coli (Escherichia coli)

Escherichia coli (E. coli) bacteria normally live in the intestines of people and animals. Most E. coli are harmless and actually are an important part of a healthy human intestinal tract. However, some variants of E. coli are pathogenic, meaning they can cause illness, either diarrhea or illness outside of the intestinal tract. The types of E. coli that can cause diarrhea can be transmitted through contaminated water or food, or through contact with animals or persons.

The time between ingesting the "Shiga toxin-producing" E. coli (aka STEC) bacteria and feeling sick is called the "incubation period." The incubation period is usually 3-4 days after the exposure, but may be as short as 1 day or as long as 10 days.

The symptoms of STEC infections vary for each person but often include:

- severe stomach cramps

- diarrhea (often bloody)

- mild fever

- and vomiting.

If there is fever, it usually is not very high (less than 101°F/less than 38.5°C). Most people get better within 5–7 days without any treatment.

Most STEC infections are very mild, but others are severe

or even life-threatening and require medical supervision to ensure a successful path to wellness.

The best treatment for STEC is hydration and general supportive therapy. Antibiotics should not be used to treat this infection.

Giardia (lamblia)

Giardia is a microscopic parasite that causes the diarrheal illness known as giardiasis. Giardia (also known as Giardia intestinalis, Giardia lamblia, or Giardia duodenalis) is found on surfaces or in soil, food, or water that has been contaminated with feces from infected humans or animals.

Giardia is protected by an outer shell that allows it to survive outside the body for long periods of time and this makes it tolerant to chlorine disinfection (i.e. chlorine purification of water alone is not enough to remove the risk of Giardia.) While the parasite can be spread in different ways, water (drinking water and recreational water) is the most common mode of transmission.

Giardiasis is the most frequently diagnosed intestinal parasitic disease in the United States and among travelers with chronic diarrhea. Signs and symptoms may vary and can last for 1 to 2 weeks or longer. In some cases, people infected with Giardia have no symptoms.

Acute symptoms include:

- Diarrhea

- Gas

- Greasy stools that tend to float

- Stomach or abdominal cramps

- Upset stomach or nausea/vomiting

- Dehydration (loss of fluids)

Other, less common symptoms include

- itchy skin

- hives

- and swelling of the eye and joints.

Sometimes, the symptoms of giardiasis might seem to resolve, only to come back again after several days or weeks. Giardiasis can cause weight loss and failure to absorb fat, lactose, vitamin A and vitamin B12.

Several drugs can be used to treat Giardia infection. Effective treatments include metronidazole, tinidazole, and nitazoxanide. Alternatives to these medications include paromomycin, quinacrine, and furazolidone.

Hepatitis A

Hepatitis A is a contagious liver disease that results from infection with the Hepatitis A virus. It can range in severity from a mild illness lasting a few weeks to a severe illness lasting several months.

Hepatitis A is usually spread when a person ingests fecal matter — even in microscopic amounts — from contact with objects, food, or drinks contaminated by the feces (or stool) of an infected person. A person can get Hepatitis A through a variety of means, including:

- Person to person contact

- When an infected person does not wash his or her hands properly after going to the bathroom and touches other objects or food – spreading the virus from bathroom surfaces to other surfaces

- When a parent or caregiver does not properly wash his or her hands after changing diapers or cleaning up the stool of an infected person

- When someone has sex or sexual contact with an infected person.

- Contaminated food or water

- Hepatitis A can be spread by eating or drinking food or water contaminated with the virus. (This can include frozen or undercooked food.) The food and drinks most likely to be contaminated are fruits, vegetables, shellfish, ice, and water. In the United States, chlorination of water kills any Hepatitis A virus that enters the water supply.

Some people with Hepatitis A do not have any symptoms. If you do have symptoms, they may include the following:

- Fever

- Fatigue

- Loss of appetite

- Nausea

- Vomiting

- Abdominal pain

- Dark urine

- Clay-colored bowel movements

- Joint pain

- Jaundice (a yellowing of the skin or eyes)

If symptoms occur, they usually appear anywhere from 2 to 6 weeks after exposure. Symptoms usually develop over a period of several days. Symptoms usually last less than 2 months, although some people can be ill for as long as 6 months.

There are no special treatments for Hepatitis A. Most people with Hepatitis A will feel sick for a few months before they begin to feel better. A few people will need to be hospitalized. During this time, doctors usually recommend rest, adequate nutrition, and fluids.

The best way to prevent Hepatitis A is through vaccination with the Hepatitis A vaccine.

Legionella (Legionnaires' Disease)

Legionella is a type of bacterium found naturally in fresh water. When people are exposed to the bacterium, it can cause illness (Legionnaires' disease and Pontiac fever). This bacterium grows best in warm water, like that found in:

- Hot tubs

- Cooling towers (air-conditioning units for large buildings)

- Hot water tanks

- Large plumbing systems

- Decorative fountains

Cooling towers use water to remove heat from a building. They are often part of the air conditioning systems of large buildings. In contrast, home and car air conditioning units do not use water to cool, so they do not aerosolize water (spread small droplets of water in the air) and are not a risk for Legionella growth.

People are exposed to Legionella when they breathe in a mist or vapor (small droplets of water in the air) containing the bacteria. One example might be from breathing in droplets sprayed from a hot tub that has not been properly cleaned and disinfected.

Less commonly, Legionella can be transmitted via aspiration of drinking water, which is when water "goes down the wrong pipe," into the trachea (windpipe) and lungs instead of down the digestive tract. People at increased risk of aspiration include those with swallowing difficulties.

Legionella cannot spread from one person to another person. A person diagnosed with Legionnaires' disease or Pontiac fever is not a threat to family members, co-workers, or others.

Legionnaires' disease can be hard to diagnose because its symptoms are similar to other types of pneumonia and it often looks the same on a chest x-ray. Specific tests are needed to determine if a case of pneumonia is Legionnaires' disease.

The most common symptoms of Legionnaires' disease include:

- Cough

- Shortness of breath

- High fever

- Muscle aches

- Headaches

These symptoms usually begin 2 to 10 days after being exposed to the bacteria, but it can take longer so people should watch for symptoms for about 2 weeks after exposure.

Legionnaires' disease requires treatment with antibiotics and most cases of Legionnaires' disease can be treated successfully. Healthy people usually get better after being sick with Legionnaires' disease, but they often need care in the hospital.

Possible complications of Legionnaires' disease include

- Lung failure

- Death

It is estimated that for every 20 people who get sick with Legionnaires' disease, between 1 and 6 will die due to complications from their illness. As you can see, it is a very serious disease.

Leptospirosis

Leptospirosis is a bacterial disease that affects humans and animals. It is caused by bacteria of the genus Leptospira. The bacteria that cause leptospirosis are spread through the urine of infected animals, which can get into water or soil and can survive there for weeks to months.

Humans can become infected through:

- Contact with urine (or other body fluids, except saliva) from infected animals.

- Contact with water, soil, or food contaminated with the urine of infected animals.

The bacteria can enter the body through skin or mucous membranes (eyes, nose, or mouth), especially if the skin is broken from a cut or scratch. Drinking contaminated water can also cause infection.

Leptospirosis can cause a wide range of symptoms,

including:

- High fever

- Headache

- Chills

- Muscle aches

- Vomiting

- Jaundice (yellow skin and eyes)

- Red eyes

- Abdominal pain

- Diarrhea

- Rash

The time between a person's exposure to a contaminated source and becoming sick is 2 days to 4 weeks. Illness usually begins abruptly with fever and other symptoms. Leptospirosis may occur in two phases:

- After the first phase (with fever, chills, headache, muscle aches, vomiting, or diarrhea) the patient may recover for a time but become ill again.

- If a second phase occurs, it is more severe; the person may have kidney or liver failure or meningitis. This phase is also called Weil's disease.

The illness lasts from a few days to 3 weeks or longer.

Without treatment, recovery may take several months.

Leptospirosis is treated with antibiotics, such as doxycycline or penicillin, which should be given early in the course of the disease. Intravenous antibiotics may be required for persons with more severe symptoms.

Norovirus

Norovirus is a very contagious virus. You can get Norovirus from an infected person, contaminated food or water, or by touching contaminated surfaces. Norovirus is the most common cause of acute gastroenteritis in the United States. Each year, it causes 19-21 million illnesses and contributes to 56,000-71,000 hospitalizations and 570-800 deaths.

Norovirus causes inflammation of the stomach or intestines or both. This is also known as acute gastroenteritis.

The most common symptoms are:

- diarrhea

- throwing up

- nausea

- stomach pain

Other symptoms may include:

- fever

- headache

- body aches

A person usually develops symptoms 12 to 48 hours after being exposed to Norovirus. Most people with Norovirus illness get better within 1 to 3 days.

There is no specific medicine to treat people with Norovirus illness. Norovirus infection cannot be treated with antibiotics because it is a viral (not a bacterial) infection.

If you have Norovirus illness, you should drink plenty of liquids to replace fluid lost from throwing up and diarrhea. This will help prevent dehydration.

Salmonella

Salmonella was discovered more than a century ago. Salmonellosis, the illness caused by Salmonella, primarily results in a mild to severe diarrheal illness, known as acute gastroenteritis.

Symptoms of acute gastroenteritis due to infection with Salmonella can include:

- Sudden onset of diarrhea (which may be bloody)

- Abdominal cramps

- Fever (almost always present)

- Nausea, vomiting, and headache may occur, though less frequent

Diarrhea may last for several days and lead to potentially severe dehydration, especially in infants and children under 2 years old and in adults over 65 years old. Even after clinical symptoms are no longer obvious, Salmonella bacteria may be found in the stool for several weeks.

Most people with diarrhea due to a Salmonella infection recover completely, although it may be several months before their bowel habits are entirely normal.

Sometimes, Salmonella infection can spread to urine, blood, bones, joints, the brain, or the nervous system, causing symptoms related to that body part or system. Some of these extra-intestinal infections can have long-term effects, depending on which part of the body is infected.

Salmonella gastrointestinal infections usually resolve, or get better, in 5-7 days. Most do not require treatment other than oral fluids. People with severe diarrhea may require rehydration with intravenous fluids.

Shigella

Shigellosis is a diarrheal disease caused by a group of bacteria called Shigella. Shigella causes about 500,000 cases of diarrhea in the United States annually. There are four different species of Shigella:

- Shigella sonnei (the most common species in the United States)

- Shigella flexneri

- Shigella boydii

- Shigella dysenteriae

S. dysenteriae and S. boydii are rare in the United States, though they continue to be important causes of disease in the developing world. Shigella dysenteriae type 1 can cause deadly epidemics.

Symptoms of shigellosis typically start 1–2 days after exposure and include:

- Diarrhea (sometimes bloody)

- Fever

- Abdominal pain

- Tenesmus (a painful sensation of needing to pass stools even when bowels are empty)

In persons with healthy immune systems, symptoms usually last about 5 to 7 days. Persons with diarrhea usually recover completely, although it may be several months before their bowel habits are entirely normal. Once someone has had shigellosis, they are not likely to get infected with that specific type again for at least several years. However, they can still get infected with other types of Shigella.

Diarrhea caused by Shigella usually resolves without antibiotic treatment in 5 to 7 days. People with mild shigellosis may need only fluids and rest. Bismuth subsalicylate (e.g., Pepto-Bismol®) may be helpful.

Typhoid

Typhoid fever is a life-threatening illness caused by the bacterium Salmonella Typhi. You can get typhoid fever if you eat food or drink beverages that have been handled by a person who is shedding Salmonella Typhi or if sewage contaminated with Salmonella Typhi bacteria gets into the water you use for drinking or washing food. Therefore, typhoid fever is more common in areas of the world where handwashing is less frequent and water is likely to be contaminated with sewage.

Once Salmonella Typhi bacteria are eaten or drunk, they multiply and spread into the bloodstream. The body reacts with fever and other signs and symptoms.

Persons with typhoid fever usually have:

- A sustained fever as high as 103° to 104° F (39° to 40° C)

- They may also feel weak

- H have stomach pains

- Headache

- Loss of appetite.

In some cases, patients have a rash of flat, rose-colored spots.

Typhoid fever is treated with antibiotics. Choices for antibiotic therapy include fluoroquinolones (for susceptible infections), ceftriaxone, and azithromycin.

Heavy Metals and Water Turbidity

The next way you can be exposed to unsafe water is turbidity – defined as the cloudiness or haziness of the water. Basically you see turbidity in the water every time there is a heavy rainfall or areas where the water is churned by the current. (Basically, the river or stream turns brown with all the fine particle debris in it.)

This disturbance stirs up contaminants in the ground beneath the water supply, and in the case of rain runoff, materials – both organic and inorganic - in the ground near streams, ponds and lakes.

Turbidity represent significant difficulties when it comes to purifying water.

1. The solids in the water making it appear hazy can contain heavy metals, pathogens and other types of contaminants that are detrimental to your health. If you live in an area where there may be heavy metals in the ground, instances of turbidity are particularly risky.

2. Turbidity decreases the effectiveness of water treatment techniques. It can protect pathogens from damage via chemical or heat treatment. It can also prevent the complete absorption of UV light if you are using that as a purification technique. And if you do not pre filter the water, it can quickly clog up any water filter system you are using to purify your water.

Groundwater Contamination

Groundwater, which includes ponds, streams, lakes, and shallow aquifers, can be contaminated by a variety of substances.

Contaminants run the gamut: gasoline and oil, pesticides, industrial toxins, fertilizers, herbicides, prescription drugs, landfill runoff, septic and sewer system leaks, etc.

According to the EPA, we should expect all water that we drink – even bottled water – will have at least trace amounts of contaminants. In other words, it would be very difficult to secure 100% pure water without a process like distillation. Obviously, we are not all dying from drinking this less than pure water. That is because the amount of contaminants in the "clean" water supplies are small enough to be harmless (or at least believed to be harmless.)

Sadly, there is no good solution here. It is part of living in our industrialized world. Whether you get your water from a city water supply, bottled water or your own well, you are by default accepting that you are ingesting some level of contaminants – many with unknown long term health effects.

A home water filtration system will help reduce your exposure. For instance, the ZeroWater Pitcher removes 95% of estrone (a form of natural estrogen), PFOA (Perfluorooctanoic acid), PFOS (perfluorooctane sulfonate), fluoxetine (a depression drug), BPA (Bisphenol A), ibuprofen; more than 80% of atrazine (a weed killer), tonalide (a synthetic musk used in perfumes, etc.), TCEP (tris(2-carboxyethyl)phosphine), DEET (an insect repellent), and almost all other drugs that may be in the water supply. It is not a perfect solution but at least it dramatically reduces the quantity of these compounds you are ingesting.

Pharmaceuticals In Water Supplies

It is a sign of the times that prescription drug use is so high in the United States and other developed countries. After all, there is huge profit to give us drugs for every form of symptom relief that the drug companies can get approved by the FDA. And it is no surprise that all the drugs are making it into our drinking water supplies. They are becoming contaminated with trace amounts of a cornucopia of drugs – a pharmacy in your tap if you will. In fact, certain people have even proposed saturating our water supply with statins since almost everyone over a certain age takes them anyways.

Drugs get into the water supply from a variety of sources: people flushing expired pills into the sewer/septic system, human waste as we urinate out excess drugs, etc.

And this stream of pollutants doesn't just stop at prescription drugs.

It also includes all the household personal care products we use. They get into the water supply as we shower them off our bodies, wash our hands, do our dishes, etc. And all those antibiotic soaps are going into the mix, helping to develop strains of resistant bacteria. Bacteria that you can later ingest and get severely ill.

Needless to say, our long term exposure effects to all these organic compounds and chemicals is not really understood. But since drugs have a huge list of side effects, you can assume that there are potential adverse effects of long term exposure – even though the daily dose level is generally quite low.

This is yet another reason it is good to have a high quality, effective water filtration system for your drinking, bathing and cooking water.

The EPA Safe Drinking Water Act

The government does want us to have safe water. I don't think they really know what that means but they make their best guess as to allowed levels of contaminants and usually take steps to make sure the entities supplying our water meet these guidelines. (But not always as in the case of the Flint, MI lead issues where a response was very slow in coming and buried in politics.)

To ensure that consumers are educated about their water supply and informed of important issues as they happen, the EPA issued a rule called the Safe Drinking Water Act. It applies to all public water systems serving 25 or more people per day.

The Safe Drinking Water Act requires water suppliers to constantly monitor their water supplies to ensure that no contaminants exceed their "safe" level as defined by the EPA. If they are exceeded, they are required to issue a safety alert.

If you live in a city, when you hear about a boil water alert on the TV or radio, you are hearing one of these required safety alerts.

I don't know about you but I consider this level of alert to be quite ineffective. It would be much better if they were required to call all their customers too because if you didn't see the alert on the TV or hear it on the radio or in the newspaper, you might not know that your water was dangerous on a particular day. It would be a simple matter for a water company to call every customer in an affected area with today's technology but that level of alert is not required by the law.

In addition to alerts, the water companies are required to supply you with annual water quality reports. These summarize all the details about the water and its safety over the past year. They highlight the "safe" levels of contaminants found in the water supply and detail any alerts that may have occurred during the year. The reports also give many other interesting details about your water supply and are worth reading to learn more about your water source.

There is obviously a lot more that can be said about toxins and contaminants in the water supply but this chapter has presented a good, detailed overview of the dangers in our water supplies – both in everyday life and in survival situations.

To learn more about water and its contaminants, please

refer to the CDC Healthy Water website at http://www.cdc.gov/healthywater/ where you can learn just about everything there is to know about water health and safety.

5 LIVING A DAY WITHOUT WATER

We all know that water is critically important to our survival and that we should have a supply of water saved for emergencies. Experts recommend stocking one gallon of water per day per person. So if you have a family of four, the experts would recommend having 40 gallons of water on hand for an emergency lasting for 10 days (1 gallon x 4 people x 10 days = 40 gallons.)

While this amount of water would certainly supply your hydration needs, it is far too little to handle all your other water needs (primarily cooking and cleanliness needs) during an emergency... something you learn when you find yourself suddenly without water.

For most of us, living without running water for even a few hours would be a unique experience. After all, even in power outages, water still flows from the municipal water supply.

But if you have a well that depends on electricity to run its pump or if something catastrophic happens to the city water infrastructure, you could find yourself without any running water for days or weeks depending on the extent of the disaster.

I've been pretty lucky. The only time I've ever been without running water was when I lived in a property with a well and lost power for 18 hours. Fortunately I has a pool so I could still flush the toilets the old fashioned way – dumping a bucket of water in a bowl – so the only hardship of the power outage was a lack of air conditioning in the hot and humid South Florida September weather.

To help you understand your true water needs in an emergency, we are going to do a thought exercise called "A Day Without Water." It examines all the points water typically touches your daily life. This thought exercise will give you a good idea how inadequate the one gallon a day per person rule really is for anything other than just a survival existence. [You may think it really isn't a problem as you can live without a shower for a few days but water is responsible for so much related to cleanliness and keeping you healthy that it quickly becomes a problem if all you have is a supply for drinking.]

To really drive the point home, it might even be good if you shut off your water supply for a day so you can truly live the experience and do more than just a thought exercise. Most houses have a shutoff valve so you can do this quite easily.

Let's look at the activities you do in your day that would

require use of your water supply:

- use the toilet

- brush teeth

- wash face

- take a shower

- wash hands

- do the dishes

- do laundry

- give your pets water

- drink water, tea, coffee, hot chocolate

- cook – pasta, rice, boiled potatoes, vegetables, etc.

- general house cleaning

- humidification in winter – which might be done with a pot of water over a wood stove since you don't have electricity

Many of these activities are typically done multiple times a day and will use up an amount of water each time.

If you start adding up all these things, you will see it adds up to quite a bit of water.

- Each toilet flush in a modern, efficient toilet will use around 1.6 gallons of water. An older toilet will require several gallons of water for an adequate flush.

- A typical short shower uses about 17 gallons of water. A bath typically uses 40 gallons.

- Cooking can easily use a gallon or more of water a day.

- Daily dish washing can use up as much as 27 gallons of water.

- Giving water to your pet(s) can use up just as much drinking water as you use yourself.

- Washing your hands, brushing your teeth, etc. can also use up several gallons throughout the day.

- Doing a load of laundry can use up as much as 40 gallons of water.

As you can see, your daily water use adds up quickly to pretty big numbers. If you are on city water, you can get a fair idea of your average daily water use from your water bill. Just look at how many gallons it says you consumed and divide that number by the number of days in the billing period. So if your family used 1,750 gallons of water over 28 days, your average water consumption is 62.5 gallons of water a day. That is more than a bathtub full of water each day.

Chances are good that you do not have that much water lying around the house – unless you have a swimming pool you can use for non food/drink purposes.

So what can you do to stretch your water supply?

You can:

- flush the toilet only when necessary.

- use wet wipes or similar products for cleaning hands and cooking surfaces.

- save water from cleaning dishes, brushing teeth and washing up to flush the toilet. Just do all your cleanliness chores in a small tub or basin and pour the dirty water in a bucket when done. When the bucket is full, you will have enough water to flush the toilet.

- do a sponge bath for general cleanliness instead of a shower and then save that water for a toilet flush.

- have a stockpile of "wet" foods that don't need extra water added to them when cooking.

- get an extra wear or two out of as many of your clothes as you can. Only wash items when they are truly dirty – and then after you wash them in the tub, use the water for toilet flushes.

- etc.

As you start to consciously think about your water use and how it can be reused/substituted, you can make plans and purchase alternate supplies to minimize your water needs in an emergency.

Keep a notebook of all your water use and your ideas on alternate methods for each particular use. This research can go a long ways towards making a water shortage experience a bit less challenging.

Remember, the whole goal of this exercise is to get you better prepared for emergencies. Treat the exercise seriously, learn from it and then make appropriate plans and purchase sufficient supplies so your family does not suffer when there is no water available to you.

6 BUILD YOUR COMPREHENSIVE WATER STORAGE PLAN

Just like creating a food storage plan to build your survival food supplies, you need to build a water storage plan to ensure that you have enough water for your needs – whether that be just for drinking or for all your water needs during an emergency situation.

The issues related to storing water are surprising similar to those for storing food:

- how much to store

- when to rotate supplies

- how to store it safely

- how to acquire more on an ongoing basis

As we have seen, there are two layers of water security – water necessary to keep you alive and water to keep you and your environment sanitary – which is an important step in keeping you healthy.

How Much Water Should You Store

You water storage program begins with determining how much water you need to store.

A large part of this decision depends on what type of disaster(s) you believe you will experience. Someone planning for a terrible winter ice storm is going to have a very different mindset and set of needs than someone planning for a major earthquake that destroys critical infrastructure that leaves you without any water, sanitation services or electricity for several weeks to months while the infrastructure get restored.

If you are prepping for a small scale situation and live in an area where you believe you will still have access to running water (but perhaps not clean running water), you can gamble and build a small water storage program. You can put aside just enough water for drinking, cooking and very basic sanitation (brushing your teeth, washing your face, etc.) In this scenario, you can manage quite well if you have enough water saved away to provide two gallons of water per family member per day.

So in this scenario, if you believe the disaster will last for 10 days and have a family of four (including pets), you should have 80 gallons of water saved (2 gallons a day * 4 people * 10 days.)

But if you are preparing for a total lack of any external supply of water, you will need to have much more put aside. In addition to the two gallons of water a day for your survival needs, you will need additional water for flushing the toilet (assuming the waste system is not damaged by the disaster), bathing, cleaning, etc.

In this scenario, you can comfortably get by with 20 gallons of extra water a day on average. With proper planning, you can get by with even less. For instance, you can flush the toilet less frequently or having access to a non flush type composting toilet, outhouse or similar arrangement – which will dramatically reduce your daily water needs. This scenario assumes that you do minimal washing of dishes and clothes and reuse water as often as possible. You do not want to waste your water resources during an emergency so reuse whenever possible is critical.

Running the numbers for that same 10 day scenario with no access to running water, you now find yourself needing 200 gallons of water to comfortably manage during this period.

When To Rotate Your Water Supplies

While water can be stored a very long time, it should still be rotated. Water sitting long enough can develop issues. Even bottled water bought at the supermarket has expiration dates stamped on them. There are a variety of reasons for this but primarily it rests with the fact that water generally has some level of contaminants that can become active again as the treatment chemicals weaken or become compromised from leaching chemicals from a container into the water. Leaching should not happen with food safe plastic containers but if stored improperly for a long time, deterioration is a possibility.

For your drinking and cooking water, a good plan is to rotate your self bottled stock every six months unless the water is treated with a water preserver to ensure that no bacteria grow in the container. If your source of water is bottled water from the supermarket, you can go by the expiration date on the bottle as long as you store it in a cool, dark place. Expiration dates on store bought water is often two to three years from the date you purchase it.

If you store water for longer than this amount of time, it is a good idea to treat it with a water purification method before drinking it. This can be accomplished by boiling, bleach treatment, a good water filter system, etc. However, if it is used for things like flushing toilets, this extra processing of old water is not necessary.

How To Store Water Safely

When you store water, you want to make sure it is stored in safe containers. Obviously, the containers you get when you purchase water at the supermarket are fine – whether they be water containers or properly cleaned one liter soda containers.

But what about if you choose to buy containers?

If you buy your own water storage containers, you want to buy containers that are FDA approved DOT #34 labeled for water storage. These containers are water stable – i.e. they do not leach any chemical residue into the water.

Note: When storing water specifically for such uses as water for flushing toilets, the quality of the container is not a real important consideration. As long as it is not for consumption, water stored in rain barrels, garbage cans, etc., can be saved and used as is. Just be sure to mark the containers with a label like "NOT FOR DRINKING" if there is any chance of someone in your family confusing your drinking supply with your other water supply.

How To Get Water In Emergencies

Water takes up a lot of space and in an ideal emergency situation you will have multiple ways planned to acquire more water for your use. You should make note of every way to acquire water near where you live and keep the appropriate supplies handy that will let you gather it and treat it so it is safe to drink.

For instance, if you have several rain collection barrels that you can tie to your roof runoff via the gutter downspouts (assuming that your city doesn't have a law against this practice), you will have a good and replenishable supply of water for non drinking purposes. (You should not drink this water unless you treat it first.) A few barrels under the various downspouts on your house can provide quite a bit of water storage.

If there is a nearby stream that runs all year, it is always a good way to get more water. It might take a bit of effort to carry the water back home but in an emergency, the effort is worth it. A few buckets or gallon containers is all you need to transport the water to your house for use or treatment.

Having a swimming pool is of course a great way to have access to extra water. And in an emergency situation, you might even be able to tap a neighbors pool for a bit of water to flush your toilets. Note that you shouldn't drink swimming pool water unless you treat it first.

While it is good to be able to collect water from sources after the fact, it is also good to pay attention to what is happening – provided there is advance warning. If a dangerous weather condition is coming, fill your bathtub(s) and any other large containers with water from your tap. Even a plastic kiddie pool is a great way to store lots of water for flushing toilets and cleaning. This extra precaution will let you go into any disaster with hundreds of extra gallons of water stored away.

Lastly, it is good to always have water purification supplies on hand so that if your drinking water supply runs low, you have the ability to purify water from other sources to drink and cook with.

As you can see, a little up front planning can go a long way towards giving you water security for almost any disaster situation that you might encounter. You don't want to have to rely on others for this basic necessity of life.

7 HOW TO TEST YOUR WATER'S SAFETY

We take it for granted that the water coming out of our tap is safe – especially if we are being supplied by a city water system.

But that is not always the case.

If you have a well, there are many things potential contaminants that can affect the quality of the water coming into your house. Even with city water, contaminants do make it into the system – sometimes in dramatic fashion as has happened in Flint Michigan and their very poor decision to save money by pulling water from the Flint river and then not treating the water with orthosphate – a chemical that lines the old pipes, keeping lead from leaching into the water. Even worse is that people in positions of authority were aware of the effects but chose to keep quiet about it to keep costs down.

While the Flint, MI case is an exceptional example of large scale water contamination, it clearly demonstrates that you need to look out for yourself – no matter how your water is supplied.

In this chapter, we explore the warning signs that suggest that you may have contaminants in your water. Knowing these warning signs will give you clues that you should have your water tested. We will also examine what contaminants can be covered by water tests and how to get your water tested.

The very first time you want to get your water tested is when you first purchase a house. At that point, it is a good idea to pay for a general water quality test. This is especially important if you are buying a house that is serviced by a well but it is good to do even if you are on a municipal water supply. The reason is that the water going into the system may be clean but by the time it gets to your faucet, it could be contaminated. There could be damaged pipes in your plumbing system affecting water quality especially if you are buying an old house tied to city water.

This basic water quality test will establish a baseline for the water that comes out of the faucet and will be your first line of defense against future water contamination.

When To Test Your Water

Once your initial water test is completed and you have been given passing grades, you can assume that your water is safe to drink. It may not taste or smell the same as the water in your last place but it is safe to drink.

If you notice changes from your baseline water taste and smell, that suggests that you might want to have a new safety test performed.

For those who get their water from a municipal water supply, a call to the water department is the first place to start if you notice differences in your water quality. From time to time, they change the ratios and concentrations of the chemicals they use to purify the water and it can impact the flavor and odor. They often do this during a heat wave and periodically to flush out the entire system.

Or there could be an algae bloom in the source water supply affecting the taste but not the safety of the water. Generally if there is a safety issue with your city water supply, they will issue an alert to the newspapers, TV and radio stations. But they are always happy to take phone calls from concerned citizens so don't hesitate to call if you have questions. They are happy to help assuage any fears you have and explain what is going on.

If you have a well, you are the only person responsible for monitoring your water quality. Here are clues to look for that suggest a new water quality test might be called for.

Any time you detect changes in the taste, smell and color of the water, you are being given strong clue that something might have changed in your water supply. Here are the most common issues you will encounter.

- A metallic taste in the water. This could be the result of fluctuations in the water table feeding your well – allowing water to be supplied from different layers. This high mineral content water can damage your pipes and if the concentration is high enough, it can cause you harm. This can generally be corrected by adding appropriate filtering components to your well system to soften the water.

- A rotten egg smell is common when there is a lot of decaying organic matter in the water table. We had this condition when we had a well in South Florida. The water was safe to drink but it smelled and tasted bad. To solve this cosmetic problem, we had to add components to our well system to aerate and lightly chlorinate the water. As an added bonus, it fed into a 300 gallon holding tank after this process so we always had a large reserve of potable water that we could access in an emergency.

  However, a rotten egg smell can also indicate the presence of unhealthy bacteria in the water. If you live in an area where this smell is not normal, you should get your water tested.

- A musty smell can indicate organic matter or pesticides leaching into your water supply. This can include organic fertilizers, farm runoff, etc. This smell is not normal and you should have a well technician come out to test and advise you of a solution.

- If you have a chemical taste in your water, it could suggest contamination by oil or gas or other industrial contaminants. These should be tested right away as they could be harmful if ingested.

- A change in the color of your water can also suggest a contaminant has entered your water supply. Many things impact the color of the water and are not necessarily harmful. For instance, rusty colored water suggests that there is manganese or iron in your water, yellow suggests your aquifer is located in a marshy or peat moss laden region, green/blue indicates that copper is in the water. And water can look cloudy due to fine particles in the water supply (also called turbidity.)

This change can often be noted when there is a long term drought, causing the water table to lower. As it lowers, it pulls water from a different part of the water supply and that can show these effects – especially turbidity of the well level is getting really low.

While a color to the water shouldn't be considered dangerous if it has always been there and has previously been tested as good, if you see a change in the color of your water, that is an indication that it should be tested.

There are other things that can affect the quality of your water that do not leave a noticeable sign. In this case, you need to pay attention to other clues. Some are detailed below.

- If you live close to a landfill, dump, chemical plant, mining operation, etc. and have an unusual event (flood, earthquake, tornado, etc.), this could stir up some pockets of contamination that could make their way into your water supply.

- You have a flood in your area that leaves standing water on top of your well cover for an extended period of time.

- You (or a neighbor) have livestock that excrete either near your well or uphill from your well.

- Your septic tank has broken or otherwise leaked and is located close to your well.

- Your family suffers bouts of gastrointestinal distress with no discernible reason.

- You work with chemicals – fertilizers, pesticides, etc. - and had an accidental spill close to your well cover.

If any of these or similar incidents occur, it is a good time to think about getting your well water tested. Tests are not that expensive and it is smart insurance to ensure the safety of your family.

Testing Your Water

There are two ways to test your water. The first is to call a professional to draw samples and process them. The second way is to buy a home test kit.

For most testing purposes, a home test kit will serve you just fine. They range in price from under $20 to over $50 and can run a pretty comprehensive test suite on your water.

For instance, the Watersafe WS425B Drinking Water Test Kit is less than $20 and can do all these tests:

- Pesticides: From Agricultural Uses. Linked to Increased Cancer Rates.

- Chlorine: By-products Can Increase Cancer Risk; Bad Taste and Smell.

- Nitrates/Nitrites: From Fertilizers and Animal Waste. Causes Development Problems.

- Pb: Lead. Causes Developmental Harm, Neurological and Kidney Damage.

- pH: Can Cause Heavy Metal (lead) Leaching, Plumbing Damage.

- Hardness: Causes Lime Scale and Higher Detergent Use.

For around $50, you can buy a First Alert WT1 Drinking Water Test Kit which runs this suite of tests:

- Bacteria: Strains of E. coli can cause serious illness or death.

- Lead: Causes developmental harm, neurological damage, and kidney damage.

- Pesticides: From agricultural uses, linked to increased cancer rates.

- Nitrates/nitrites: From fertilizers and animal waste, causes developmental problems.

- Chlorine: By-products can increase cancer risk and cause bad taste and odor.

- Hardness: Causes lime scale and higher detergent use.

- pH: Can cause heavy metal (such as lead) leaching and

plumbing damage.

A water technician can't really do much more than these tests on the spot and it will certainly cost you much more for them to do the testing.

But a water technician can spot other problems and can suggest tests that aren't covered by the typical water test kits you can buy. They can also send the water sample to professional labs that can run a suite of about 100 contaminant related tests on your water supply. While this may seem really comprehensive, it will give you a complete analysis of your water and any problems.

You should always have your first water test done by a water technician when you buy your house – and insist on a comprehensive lab test. Once you know the water is safe, the store bought test kits are generally fine unless an event occurs that makes you worry about possible damage to your well system or unusual contamination that is not tested in store bought kits.

And if you have a well, it is essential to have a water technician do the first inspection/test to be sure everything in the well system is working and in good shape as well as ensuring that your water supply is clean. You want to be sure all the components of the well are in good condition and doing their job properly. It is not uncommon to buy a house with a well and find the filtration system is no longer performing as it should.

The bottom line is if you ever have any doubts about your water safety, call in the experts. We need water every day and we want to be sure it is safe.

8 HOW TO PURIFY WATER

Unless you live in an extreme desert climate or are in an area experiencing a deep, long drought, you can probably find sources of water. They might be streams, ponds, puddles, runoff from your roof after a rain, underground sources, etc.

Whatever the source, they all have one thing in common. They should be considered dirty water and it would be advisable to purify the water from these sources before using it for drinking. It is also good purify it before cooking because even though cooking implies boiling which would destroy biological contaminants, it won't do anything about other types of contaminants or particles in the water source. Methods to purify water include:

- filtering

- boiling

- chemical treatment

- distillation

- reverse osmosis

- UV light treatment

- and many other methods

If is best if you can combine methods to produce the cleanest water possible. For instance, if the water is cloudy, you should prefilter it to remove all the large particles before running it through your primary water filter, boiling or chemical treatment. The end result will be much better and if you are using a filter, it will give it a much longer life as those larger particles will quickly clog it and dramatically reduce its effectiveness.

This chapter explores the various methods of treating water. It discusses their pros and cons and supplies other details you need to know to ensure that your drinking water supply will not make you sick.

Each water purification method provides some degree of protection from biological and chemical contaminants. By understanding how the various methods work and what they can do, you can make informed equipment decisions for your family based on the potential sources of water that would be available to you in an emergency.

Water Filters & Purifiers

The first type of water treatment method we will discuss is water filters and purifiers.

Water filters and purifiers are devices that take impure water in at one end and deliver better quality water at the other end. When people discuss water filters, they generally lump water filters and water purifiers in the same category. But from a technical perspective, filters and purifiers are very different devices – and perform very different actions on your unclean water. It is important to understand the differences before buying a water treatment system.

A water filter is the term used for any device that removes impurities from the water. By this definition, a coffee filter is a water filter. But in practical terms, if you buy a product labeled a water filter, it generally means that it passes water through a membrane fine enough to remove protozoa and certain classes of bacteria. A filter does not remove very small organic compounds, inorganic compounds like heavy metals, minerals or salts. It only removes particles of a size that is larger than the holes in the membrane.

A water purifier is a special class of water treatment device that meets very specific EPA specifications. EPA defines a purifier as a device that reduces all pathogens in the water supply to a safe level. This means that it removes at least 99.9999% of all bacteria, 99.99% of all viruses and 99.9% of all Cryptosporidium in the water. Therefore, if you see a mechanism advertised as a water purifier, it has to meet these requirements.

As you can see, paying attention to the specifications of your water treatment system is important so you understand exactly what it will deliver. Also note that in neither case is there a requirement to remove heavy metals, minerals or salts from the water. Filters and purifiers are strictly related to removing particles and organic contaminants from the water. That said, there are more complete filtration systems that also handle the inorganic compounds but from a strict definition point, filters and purifiers do not work with inorganic compounds.

Your most common experience with water filters/purifiers are systems that either attach to your faucet or pitchers with a filter of some sort built into them. They are all designed to work with your tap water. The ZeroWater pitcher system is an excellent choice for delivering really clean water from your tap. It removes just about everything from the water – meaning that if your well gets a contaminant or your city issues a boil water alert, this system probably has you covered. It is probably the best of the water filter systems you can buy at your local store. Other options are PUR and Brita but their filtration systems are not quite as comprehensive.

But if you are in a situation where you do not have running water but rather have to rely on an outside source – pond, stream, etc. - you should take a few additional steps before using your portable water filter system.

First, you should prefilter your water. Prefiltering will remove all the large debris from the water – debris that could clog your purifier and render it inoperable very quickly. This prefilter can be something as simple as pouring water from one bucket to another using a cotton shirt as a filter to get rid of large particles or as complex as a multi-layer affair where each layer catches more and smaller debris.

The next step (if you have to equipment to do it) would be to check and adjust the pH level of the water if you have the ability to do that. Some water sources are very acid or alkaline. This imbalance can affect the performance of your water purification system. Having the basic chemicals and testing equipment to make your water pH neutral will dramatically extend the life of your system.

Note: This is an area of prepping where it is good to have already identified outside sources of water near your home. It gives you an opportunity to collect and experiment with samples of these water supplies before you need them. By experimenting, you will be able to make the best equipment decisions for working with your most likely emergency sources.

Once you do that, you have a good source of water to introduce to your purification system – whether it be a ZeroWater system or something like a Big Berkey or Katadyn pocket pump or one of the other well rated systems.

Water filters can be commercially bought or hand made. If you are looking at a purifier (and you should), it would generally have to be a commercial product as you cannot build a system that can filter to that degree with homemade materials. However, your homemade system can be combined with boiling or chemical purification to get excellent results.

Homemade systems are quite easy to construct and use only a few basic materials. If you do a search on the internet for "how to build a homemade water filter", you will find many illustrated instruction guides to help you succeed in this project.

Reverse osmosis systems

The next class of filtration system is reverse osmosis. To understand this way this type of system works, you first need to understand the process of osmosis.

Osmosis is defined as a process which allows molecules to pass through a semipermeable membrane from a less concentrated solution into a more concentrated one, thus equalizing the concentration of the molecules on each side of the membrane.

A good example of this process is what happens when one is drinking salt water. We all know it is bad and that if you drink enough, it can dehydrate you. And the process that causes the dehydration is osmosis.

Your body is pumping water into your stomach to try to lower its salinity to a safe level – i.e. it is taking water from your body (a low salt concentration region) and putting it into your stomach (a high salt concentration region) to balance the salt levels in your stomach with your body. And as it takes water out of your body, it is causing you to become dehydrated.

Reverse osmosis is simply the reverse of this process. It removes high concentrates and discharges low concentrates. This is accomplished by forcing pressurized water through a very fine membrane, discharging the excess concentrate filled water. In the case of a reverse osmosis filtration system, the concentrates are the various pollutants in the water.

A reverse osmosis system is typically a multistage system comprised of four parts. It has a pre-filter, a semi-permeable membrane, a pressurized storage tank for the filtered water and a carbon post processing filter.

Reverse osmosis systems are excellent at removing all pathogens as well as a large variety of chemical impurities. While this sounds like a perfect system, there are many reasons it is not an ideal system for prepping – or even for everyday home use for your well supplied water.

The reasons include:

1. The system needs a high pressure water intake to work. Typical systems need an intake of at least 40psi of water pressure to work. No home based system has that level of pressure. Typical well and municipal water systems supply water at 40 to 80psi. To reach the 400psi level, you need a supplemental electric pump to raise the pressure. And that means the system is not going to work if you do not have power.

2. Reverse osmosis systems waste a tremendous amount of water. For each gallon of treated water, you will actually use 10 to 15 gallons of water – with the rest being wasted.

3. It does require periodic maintenance and replacement of

parts. Now all filtration systems require replacement of parts from time to time but because of the more complex nature of a reverse osmosis system, you are more likely to need professional assistance than with more traditional filtration systems.

However, reverse osmosis is one of the few processes that can make seawater drinkable – so if your alternate water source is salty marsh water or brackish bay water, you may want to look into a portable reverse osmosis system powered by a solar energy source. While this use sounds exotic, they are actually quite commonly used in more expensive boats to supply water for long trips.

Chemical Purification

The next method of purification is chemical treatment of the water. This is generally accomplished with bleach, iodine, silver or hydrogen peroxide. The next several sections will examine each of these chemical treatments and their benefits.

Bleach/Chlorine

Chlorine is the most common commercial method of treating municipal water supplies because it is hugely effective in that controlled environment. [Note: Many municipalities now use a salt based treatment system that generates chlorine ions rather than adding chlorine concentrate to the water supply. You can purchase a similar system for your swimming pool.]

When it comes to treating water in a personal level, chlorine is a very effective option but there are potential issues you need to be aware of. They are:

- Chlorine will react with organic materials in the water, attaching itself to the nitrogen containing compounds, leaving less free chlorine to continue disinfecting the water. This means that the recommended dose might not give the effect you expect. This process is mitigated if the water is filtered beforehand to remove most organic compounds. In other words, the best water to treat with chlorine is water that is already clear. [Note that clear does not mean not contaminated.]

- Super chlorination will ensure that enough chlorine was used but makes the resulting water unfit for drinking after treatment. However if you practice super chlorination, you can filter the water through an activated charcoal filter or add hydrogen peroxide to neutralize the excess chlorine in the water. If this method is used, the water must be used very quickly as the processes will remove all chlorine from the water and allow it to become recontaminated if it sits for too long. In other words, superchlorination followed by immediate filtering is not a good solution for stabilizing water for long term storage.

  As a side note: If you have a swimming pool, you are super chlorinating it when you open it at the beginning of the season and add pool shock to it.

- Chlorine is pH and temperature sensitive. If the temperature of the water is cold, the chlorine will work more slowly. If the pH is greater than 8, the effectiveness of chlorination drops dramatically. And if the pH is low, the chlorine will form hypochlorous acid rather than neutralize contaminants.

As long as the above items are not significant issues for you, chlorination can be a very safe and effective means of purifying biologically contaminated water.

How to purify water with bleach

The most common approach to purify water with bleach is to use standard household bleach you would buy at the supermarket. Be sure that you buy bleach with no additives or perfumes. Pure household bleach contains a 5-6% solution of sodium hypochlorite. If the bleach lists any other ingredients, scents or colorings, you cannot use the product to purify your water. You must use pure bleach – like regular Chlorox.

Bleach is chemically unstable so it will slowly lose its strength – meaning that as it ages, you will need to use more and more to purify your water. Because it is unstable, you should rotate your supply of bleach to keep it as fresh as possible and ready when an emergency arises. But even old bleach can still do the job. You will just need to use more.

Assuming your bleach is relatively fresh, here is the procedure for treating your water supply.

1. If the water is cloudy, you should filter it before treatment. This can often be adequately accomplished by running it through several layers of clean cloth.

2. Pour the water to be disinfected into a known size container. This is important to know how much chlorine to

add to it.

3. Allow the water to warm up to room temperature if possible. Room temperature is generally considered in the high 60's to the low 70s in degrees Fahrenheit. If you can't warm it up, that is OK (and will be addressed in another step below.)

4. Add the bleach. The formula is 2 drops per quart (8 drops for a gallon container.) This is why you want to know the size of your container. If the water is cloudy, you will want to add more bleach – generally a double dose – 16 drops per gallon.

5. Stir the bleach into the water and let it sit for 30 minutes. If the water is cold/cloudy, you should let the water sit for 60 minutes.

6. After the appropriate amount of time has passed, you should still be able to faintly smell bleach in the water. If you cannot, you did not add enough bleach and the water should be treated again before being used.

As a final safeguard, you may want to get a chlorine test kit. The goal of water purification with bleach is to have a residual chlorine level of 0.2 to 0.5 mg/l thirty minutes after dosing the water. Once you hit that point, you can be sure the water is safe to use. Kits are relatively inexpensive and make a good addition to your supplies – but like many things, they do expire so you should plan on checking and replacing as necessary.

If you are like most people, you do not like the chlorine

taste in the water. You can get rid of the smell/taste by letting the water sit a while longer. This will let the rest of the smell and taste of the chlorine evaporate from the water. If you do this, be sure to use the water quickly (i.e. within a few days) after the chlorine smell dissipates to prevent recontamination. And if you don't like the taste of the treated water, adding a few drops of lemon/lime juice or a small amount of powdered drink mix goes a long way towards fixing that problem.

Amount of Chlorine to use for specific volumes of water

Water Quantity	Clear Water	Cloudy Water
1 Quart	2 Drops	4 drops
1 Gallon	8 Drops	16 drops
5 Gallons	1/2 teaspoon	1 teaspoons
10 Gallons	1 teaspoon	2 teaspoons
55 Gallons	5 1/2 teaspoons	11 teaspoons

Iodine

Iodine is considered more effective than chlorine at purifying water as it is not as sensitive to the pH or the organic content of the water. This removes the bit of trial and error which applies when purifying with bleach.

Iodine follows the same purifying process as bleach as

described above with only minor differences:

- You will use 3 drops of iodine per quart of water (12 drops per gallon.)

- Your water will have a reddish/brown color to it from the iodine. This is normal and does not affect the potability of the water supply.

- You will taste the iodine in the water. It doesn't evaporate like bleach does. Vitamin C removes the taste of the iodine from water so a bit of powdered up vitamin C or a flavored drink powder with vitamin C added will make the water much more palatable.

Amount of Iodine to use for specific volumes of water

Water Quantity	Clear Water	Cloudy Water
1 Quart	5 Drops	10 drops
1 Gallon	20 Drops	½ teaspoon
5 Gallons	1 teaspoon	2 teaspoons
10 Gallons	2 teaspoons	4 teaspoons
55 Gallons	11 teaspoons	22 teaspoons

Silver

While it may sound strange, silver can be used to purify water. The EPA doesn't approve of silver as a water purification method because in VERY high levels, it can cause argyrosis – a blue/gray staining of the eyes, skin and mucous membranes. But you would have to work very hard with any silver water treatment to get this level of exposure. At the EPAs maximum exposure level of 50 ppb (parts per billion) daily dose, you would have to take that dose for 27 years build up a level in your body sufficient to develop argyrosis.

While you can cobble together a silver system using silver nitrate or a colloidal silver suspension, the easiest way to work with silver based purification is to use the Katadyn Micropur tablets which contains both chlorine and silver ions.

They are a great way to kill bacteria in water and protect the water for as long as six months. Here are the details from Katadyn:

- Micropur prevents the growth of germs and the development of smells in drinking water containers and pipes.

- The effect of Micropur is based on the bacteriostatic and bactericidal properties of silver. Unlike chlorine, which is only effective for a few hours in water, silver ions will preserve water for up to 6 months. The silver ions cling to the cell walls of micro-organisms thus hindering their growth.

- Use for clear, not for cloudy water as suspended matter can weaken the effect of silver ions. If you have cloudy water, you should filter it before using Micropur.

- Micropur has a stable shelf life of 10 years making it an excellent product for your long term storage program.

Coagulant/Flocculation Agents

The last area of chemical purification to examine is coagulant/flocculation agents. These chemical agents help clarify the water by "clumping" all the fine particles until they are heavy enough to sink to the bottom of the water supply.

While their primary purpose is clumping fine particles and making them heavy enough to settle to the bottom of the water vessel, they do have a secondary beneficial effect. Some portion of the bacteria in the water will be attached to these fine particles and end up settling on the bottom. This means that there is less bacteria in the water at the time of treatment. So even though this process does not kill bacteria, it reduces the levels of bacteria in the water.

Also, by removing fine particles in the water, chlorine treatment of the water will be much more effective. As you recall, cloudy water dramatically reduces the effectiveness of chlorine treatment of water so this is a perfect compliment to chlorine treatment.

The typical flocculation agent is alum. It is mixed with the water at a ratio of approximately 20 mg per liter of water. The water is then stirred for five minutes to ensure that the alum is evenly distributed throughout the water. After 30 minutes, the particulate matter will have settled to the bottom of the container and the clear water can be poured out of the container for further treatment.

Heat

The next way to sanitize water is by the application of heat. There are many ways to do this: pasteurization, boiling, using a solar still and using a distillation apparatus.

Heating water works to purify it by raising the temperature high enough to kill microorganisms in it. The same process is used in dairy milk and many similar products in a process called pasteurization.

So what is pasteurization?

Pasteurization is a gentle heating process designed to reduce the number of viable microorganisms in a liquid to the point where they are rendered harmless. It is a technique that has been used for decades to lengthen the shelf life of milk and more recently is used to treat a wide variety of liquids – including juices.

The technique is really simple. All you do is gently heat the liquid (in this case water) to just over 149 degrees Fahrenheit and then maintain that temperature for at least one minute. Once you do that, the water is considered pasteurized and has been rendered safe from any microorganisms that may be lurking in the unpasteurized water.

So if it only takes 150 degrees to make the water potable, why does everyone say to boil the water?

When water boils, we get a visual indicator that it is at a certain temperature (212 degrees Fahrenheit.) Unless you have a temperature measurement device – a thermometer or a water pasteurization indicator (WAPI) – the bubbles generated by boiling water are the only sure visual indicator that the water has indeed hit the 150 degree threshold to become pasteurized.

Therefore, it is always a good idea to boil water to be sure it is safe when you have no other way to test if pasteurization has occurred.

Since we know boiled water is safe, why even worry about pasteurization?

It all comes down to energy. It takes a lot less energy to reach 150 degrees than it does to reach 212 degrees. So if you can pasteurize your water instead of boil it, you can dramatically stretch how long your stored cooking fuel source will last.

And testing for pasteurization is really simple to do. All you need is a cooking thermometer. Any sort of candy or meat thermometer will do the trick. Just heat it until the thermometer reads at least 150 degrees and then be sure it stays at that temperature or higher for at least one minute.

But if you don't have a thermometer, always take the safe route and let the water boil. As you saw from the chapter on waterborne diseases, a wrong guess by eyeballing the water could get you sick.

In addition to boiling over a heat source to purify it, we have another heat based method that will produce drinking water: distillation.

Distillation is the process of evaporating the water supply and then condensing it back into water. There are two ways to generate distilled water. The first is to apply heat to boil the water into steam and then cooling the steam back into liquid water with cooling coils. The second method is using a solar still which evaporates the water at lower than boiling point and then condenses the vapor back into water.

Distillation with a heat source starts with a still. A still basically consists of a pot that holds the water to be boiled and a set of cooling coils that fit over the top of the pot to capture the steam and cool it back into water which drips into a collection pot. If you've ever seen pictures of a moonshine rig on TV, that is what a still looks like. Although modern water distillers are much more compact and clean looking than the old moonshine stills in the movies.

Home water distillers generally use electricity as their heat source to boil the water and run a fan that helps cool the steam in the cooling coils. These are not really useful in a survival situation. But there is one home distiller that runs on any heat source – like on a gas stove or an open flame. That distiller is the Waterwise 1600 Non-Electric Distiller. It can generate up to 16 gallons of distilled water a day – more than enough for your family's needs.

The second method of distilling water is by using a solar still. Solar stills are very simple to build but they do need sunshine to power them. A solar still can be used to get water from wet ground, plants or water.

A typical solar still involves a plastic sheet which covers a hole in the ground filled with your water source (damp ground, nonpoisonous plant matter, dirty water, etc.) The center of the plastic sheeting is weighted down with a stone so you have a funnel shaped piece of plastic sheeting. Directly below the stone, on the underside of the plastic sheet, you place your capture container.

As the sun shines on the still, the area under the plastic sheet heats up causing evaporation of your water source to occur. The evaporated water hits the plastic, condenses and drips down the funnel into the container. Note that the water is condensing and dripping on the side of the plastic sheet closest to the hole – not the top part of the plastic.

A solar still doesn't produce a huge amount of water but it takes little effort to set up one or more of them and the still does not use any of your energy supplies like the other methods. Setting up a few of these stills on a sunny day can really help in an emergency. The downside is that this method will not really work when the weather is freezing and/or cloudy.

Since all you need to create a solar still is a sheet of plastic, it is a good idea to keep a few sheets on hand just in case. It is pretty cheap insurance if you live in an area that gets lots of sun.

Light

The next way to purify water is with light. There are two ways: a UV light source and long term exposure to sunlight in a closed container.

UV Light Systems

UV light systems rely on ultraviolet light to kill pathogens in your water. The wavelength of the UV light is harmful to all pathogens – killing many outright. But in some instance, it is not effective. It will not usually work for protozoan cysts and Giardia – but these types of contaminants are easily filtered out with a mechanical filter due to their comparatively large size.

UV treatment works best on clear water. If your water is hazy or cloudy, you will not get good penetration of the UV wavelength light throughout the water and it can leave pockets of the water untreated. Therefore if you do use a UV filter as a purification method, be sure the water is clear before applying. Prefiltering or using a flocculation agent first is recommended for sources exhibiting any amount of turbidity.

There are several commercial UV treatment systems available – many at low cost. Some are hand powered – like the SteriPen Sidewinder Hand Powered UV Water Purifier with a built in prefilter to remove turbidity from the water.

This is a very quick water treatment process – generating safe, drinkable water in minutes.

Sunlight Treatment

Another way to treat water is regular sunlight shining through a closed, clear container. The process is called solar water disinfection (SODIS).

Exposure to sunlight has been shown to deactivate diarrhea-causing organisms in polluted drinking water. Three effects of solar radiation are believed to contribute to the inactivation of pathogenic organisms:

- UV-A radiation from the sun interferes directly with the metabolism and destroys cell structures of bacteria.

- UV-A (wavelength 320–400 nm) reacts with oxygen dissolved in the water and produces highly reactive forms of oxygen (oxygen free radicals and hydrogen peroxides) that are believed to also damage pathogens.

- Cumulative solar energy (including the infrared radiation component) heats the water in the container – speeding the disinfection process.

On a typical summer day, it can take from five to eight hours to disinfect water in a clear container. So this is a slow process but it is effective.

Here are the steps involved:

1. Use a clean, colorless, transparent PET water or soda pop bottle (2 litre or smaller size). Glass bottles will not work. Remove all labels and wash the bottles before the first use.

2. Fill the bottles with water from contaminated source. Make sure it is as clean as water possible. If there is turbidity, be sure to filter the water to remove solid impurities. You can make a simple funnel filter from cloth stretched over inverted bottle cut in half. Or use a flocculation agent to settle any turbidity and then pour the clear water into the containers.

3. While not required, improving oxygen saturation in the bottles can be beneficial. Fill the bottles three-quarters full, shake for 20 seconds (with the cap on), then fill the rest of the way and recap the bottle.

4. The filled bottles are then exposed to the Sun. Bottles will heat faster and to higher temperatures if they are placed on a sloped Sun-facing dark surfaces. Placing bottles on a slightly curved sheet of aluminum foil increases UV light inside the bottle. Ensure bottles are not shaded at any time during the treatment.

5. The treated water can be consumed directly from the bottle or poured into clean drinking cups. The risk of re-contamination is minimized if the water is stored in the bottles. Storage in other containers increases the risk of contamination.

That's all you need to do. It is a great and really inexpensive way to get supplemental clean water.

Homemade Filters

You can build a variety of homemade filters/water systems to clean water. They work with varying degrees of success.

We will examine some of the more popular ones and let you know exactly what they can do for you.

[**Note**: If you search for any of these filters with your favorite search engine, you will find plenty of tutorials and illustrations to help you construct your own filter.]

Transpiration/Vegetation Bag

The first class of systems we will look at is what is known as the transpiration (aka vegetation) bag filter. This method relies on sunlight as its agent and the fact that vegetation contains locked in water that can be extracted under the right circumstances.

Building a vegetation bag water extraction system is pretty easy and only takes a few parts: a large, clear plastic bag, a rock, some tubing, non-poisonous plant matter and sunlight.

To build the system, you fill the bag roughly 50-70% full with your vegetation. Then you place a rock in it to form a well in the bottom of the bag and place one end of your tubing next to the rock. Tightly seal the bag with a knot – being sure that the other end of the tubing is extended outside of the bag through the knot so that there are no rips in the bag. Visually, think of the plastic bag as a cup with a cover and the plastic tube as a straw that goes to the bottom of the cup.

Then you want to place the bag into a really sunny spot – keeping the rock at the lowest point. You can lay it on a sloped piece of land or hang it with a piece of rope. As the sunlight hits the bag, it will heat up and cause evaporation of the plant, forcing them to release their moisture – which will then condensation into water on the surface of the plastic. This condensate will drip down to the lowest point (where you have your rock and one end of your drinking tube) and you can use the tube to drink from the reservoir of water that is formed. Depending on the amount of sunlight and the types of plants used, this method can produce water for a few days before needing new plant matter.

If you have the equipment, this is a good way to generate a survival amount of water. It will not produce huge quantities but every little bit of pure, clean drinking water is precious when you are trying to survive.

If you do not have a hose, you can just carefully open the bag, pour out the water and reseal the bag. Just take care that you do not rip the bag.

The difference between a vegetation bag and a transpiration bag is that you are working with living plants in the transpiration bag – usually bushes and trees. This method allows you to keep reusing the same portion of a bush/tree every few days. Other than that, it works identically to a vegetation bag.

This method will not generate a large quantity of water but if you can set up several vegetation bags, the cumulative amount of water generated can be sufficient to meet your needs.

Slow Sand Filter

A slow sand filter is a small scale version of an industrial sand filter adapted for household use. The filter consists of layers of sand and gravel in a concrete or plastic container approximately 0.9 meters tall and 0.3 meters square. The water level is maintained to 5-6 cm above the sand layer by setting the height of the outlet pipe.

This shallow water layer allows a bioactive layer to grow on top of the sand, which contributes to the reduction of disease-causing organisms. A diffuser plate is used to prevent disruption of the biolayer when water is added. To use the filter, users simply pour water into the top, and collect finished water out of the outlet pipe into a bucket. Over time, especially if source water is turbid, the flow rate can decrease. Users can maintain flow rate by cleaning the filter through agitating the top level of sand, or by pre-treating turbid water before filtration.

Slow sand filter lab effectiveness studies with a mature biolayer have shown 99.98% protozoan, 90-99% bacterial, and variable viral reduction. Field effectiveness studies have documented E. coli removal rates of 80-98% which is what you should expect if you use such a filter.

These filters are high maintenance. If they are not fed a continuous supply of water, the biolayer can dry out and die off – rendering the filter relatively ineffective until it restores itself. However, if you have a way to constantly feed it clear water to keep the biolayer alive, it can be a good source of drinking water for your daily use.

If you are interested in learning more about this filtering technique, please visit the slow sand filter website at http://www.slowsandfilter.org/index.shtml.

As you can see, there are many ways to ensure water safety in an emergency situation but they all require preplanning and having the appropriate supplies on hand before a disaster. Therefore, you should research the method(s) that will work best in any situations you envision you and your family encountering and then equip your gear with the appropriate solutions. In this way, you can be assured of delivering safe water to your family no matter what may happen in the future.

9 LONG TERM WATER STORAGE

Long term water storage is a big challenge for most people. While it is quite easy to buy several 24 packs of water from the supermarket for an upcoming weather disaster, it becomes more challenging when planning for longer term events. When you consider space considerations, rotation, having the necessary equipment to treat risky water supplies, etc., the idea of storing more than a few packs of water becomes daunting.

This chapter will help demystify the challenges and help you build a long term water storage plan that works for you.

As you have learned in previous chapters, you need to have a massive supply of water stored for a long term disaster – and this takes up a large amount of space. Or you need to identify and be ready to use an alternative source of water. This could be a solar power system for a well on your property, large storage tanks or purification equipment and buckets to pull water from a nearby pond or stream. It could even include making advance decisions such as installing a several thousand gallon cistern on your property or even installing a pool or a roof water capture system (if allowed by your local government) as an emergency storage system.

This chapter examines all the issues related related to storing water for long periods – from storage systems to treatment to stabilize the water long term to effectively using and rotating the water in your storage program.

Water Storage Guidelines

Before you begin storing water, there are some important safety guidelines regarding containers and storage locations that you will want to follow to maximize safety.

Improper storage containers can leech harmful chemicals into your water, making you sick if exposed long term. To avoid that, take the following steps:

- Store your water only in food grade storage containers, preferably FDA approved DOT #34 opaque containers to minimize light intrusion although any food grade container is   acceptable.

   A food grade water storage container defined as a container that will not transfer noxious or toxic substances into the water it is holding. And it is stable so this applies whether it holds water for a week or several years.

If you are uncertain whether a storage container you are thinking of using is food grade, you can contact the manufacturer. Ask if that particular container is (US) FDA approved - meaning that it is safe for food use. Alternatively, many containers contain markings identifying them as food grade. For a full description of the markings you can find on containers, refer to this article: http://theweekendprepper.com/food-storage/how-to-tell-if-your-containers-are-food-safe/

- Whether you have brand new containers or are reusing old containers, it is essential that you clean all water containers before you fill them. The procedure is simple and is described below.

    1. Wash the storage container with dish washing soap and water and rinse completely with clean water.

    2. Sanitize the container with a solution made by mixing 1 teaspoon of unscented liquid household chlorine bleach in one quart of water. Be sure it is pure bleach. That means no scents or other additives.

    3. Cover the container and shake it well so that the sanitizing bleach solution touches all inside surfaces of the container.

    4. Wait at least 30 seconds to let it work and then pour the sanitizing solution out of the

container.

   5. Let the empty sanitized container air-dry before use OR rinse the empty container with clean, safe water that is available already.

- Once you have adequately cleaned your containers, fill them with a known clean water source. This can be tap water or water that you have treated to make sure it is clean.

- Put a fill date/expiration date label on the container so you know when to replace/retreat it. Stored water should not be kept for more than six months unless it was pretreated with a water preserver. If so treated, it will allow the water to sit much longer than the six month standard. The documentation that comes with the water preserver will let you know how long the water will stay stable after being treated.

- Store your water containers in a dark location, far away from potential contaminants like pesticides, pest intrusion areas, paint, gasoline or other chemicals.

- Keep your stored water in a place with a fairly constant cool temperature (50-70° F) if at all possible. Definitely do not store it in a place where it can freeze. Freezing can damage your containers, causing leaks and potential for contamination to enter through any cracks that were created.

It is recommended that you build your water storage

program with a combination of small and large containers. The small containers are good for daily use and the large containers are good for refilling the small containers. For instance, a 55 gallon drum of water is not easy to work with. However, if you install a hand pump into the drum, you are now able to extract small portions into smaller containers that are much easier to work with on a day to day basis.

When it comes to storing water in large containers, you should consider adding a concentrated water preserver like 7Cs Water Preserver. This product will keep the water stable and microorganism free for up to five years – making it a perfect addition to add to your large water drums. You can learn more about this product from the manufacturer at their website http://www.waterpreserver.com/.

Examples of safe containers

There are many safe containers available for your water storage needs. Chances are you already have a supply of small containers coming into your house every week that can be repurposed for convenient water storage – great for daily use in an emergency. You can just clean them as described above, fill them with potable water and add them to your water cache.

Various types of containers include:

- Gallon water containers

- Five gallon water containers

- Two liter soda bottle containers

- Large glass containers. While these are excellent containers, they are heavy and can shatter so consider that before stocking up on them.

- Any of a wide variety of water safe containers from a sports store or online. They come in a variety of sizes from a few gallons up to hundreds of gallons. Just go to your favorite search engine and type in **water safe storage containers** and you will find a variety of choices from the reasonably priced WaterBOB to slightly more expensive but very high quality water barrels to huge storage tanks and multi thousand gallon cisterns.

Examples of unsafe containers

There are a wide variety of unsafe storage containers – basically any container that isn't labeled as food safe. For example, you do not to store water in a bleach container or a large laundry detergent container.

Basically any container that is not marked food grade should not be used for water storage. The material that the container is made from will leach into the water and contaminate it.

Additionally, there are other situations where you would want to reject food grade containers.

1. If your food container stored a non food item for any period of time, you want to reject that container. You can

never be if it affected the integrity of the container with contaminants that cannot be removed by following the cleaning process.

2. Milk and juice containers (unless glass) also should be rejected. Even though the containers are food safe, it is almost impossible to completely remove the fruit sugars or milk proteins from these containers. And if there is any of this sort of contaminant in the container, it can promote bacteria growth when water is stored in them for any length of time. Basically the sugars and proteins can spoil and/or act as a food source for any microorganisms that might still be in the water supply.

Dispensing water

One thing that most people don't think about in advance is how to work with their stored water supply on a daily basis when there is no power – especially when the bulk is in large storage containers.

Some of this is common sense. If you have soda bottles or even five gallon containers used for your water storage containers, they can be used as is. The five gallon containers are awkward but you can use them to fill smaller container – even if it takes two people to do the job. There are plenty of wide mouth dispensers that can be filled pretty easily or you can get a water dispenser made for the five gallon containers that works on gravity so no electricity is required.

But what about the larger containers – like 55 gallon drums? They are too large to lift and you do not want to be opening a big lid and dipping in a bucket – potentially contaminating the supply.

In this scenario, you will want to be sure your large containers are compatible with a siphon pump. With a siphon pump, you never open the container. You just work the mechanical pump mechanism and water comes out. And when one barrel is empty, you just move the pump to another barrel and you are good to go. Many of the large containers are specially designed to have a small cover that can be removed to allow for the insertion of this pump – maintaining a tight seal and keeping your water good as you use it over the next several days/weeks.

Fortunately, almost every type of barrel or large storage system is set up to take a siphon pump. Just be sure to inquire when making your purchase to be sure you get a pump that is most compatible with your barrels.

In real life, a system of this type is quite easy to use. Just carry some small, empty containers to your tank, put the pump hose in the small container and pump until it is full. Depending on the size of your family, you may need to make a few trips a day to your bulk water storage area but it is a very simple and easy to manage your water needs.

Solutions

There are many homemade and commercial solutions for your water storage needs. This section breaks them down by size to help you focus your research efforts in meeting your storage needs. Please do your own research to find the products that best fit your needs. Several suggested

Steven Chabotte

commercial products are in the Appendix to give you a starting point for your own research.

Small scale storage

Small scale storage is basically portable water – water you can generally move from one place to another by yourself. This includes all storage methods up to and including five gallon containers (which weigh about 40 pounds.)

Your best source for this form of storage container is your local supermarket or big box department store. These stores let you buy water in a variety of sizes, including 16 ounce plastic bottles, one gallon containers, 2.5 and 5 gallon containers as well as 2 liter soda bottles and similar containers that can be cleaned and reused.

Small scale storage containers from the store are really convenient and should provide a cornerstone of your water storage program. Many of them are already pretreated to have a long storage life. For instance, the 24 pack of 16.9 ounce containers I buy have a shelf life of over four years. The only problem with small storage containers is that they take up a lot more space than large containers – making it impractical to store a huge supply in this manner. But if you do have a large, cool storage area, you can store several months worth of water in this format.

If you use this water just for drinking (and not for cleaning or sanitation needs), a relatively small supply can go a long way. Each 24 pack of 16 ounce bottles holds three gallons of water – enough for one person to have enough water for six days of

126

drinking ½ gallon a day – plenty to stay fully hydrated in almost any scenario.

Medium scale storage

Medium scale storage solutions are products like water barrels and unique products like the WaterBOB - which is a plastic container that fits in your bathtub.

A WaterBOB is pretty nice to have when you can get in front of a weather emergency because it is flexible plastic bottle that folds up into a very small size. When you use it, you place it in the bathtub and as it fills, it basically fills the entire bathtub as it expands with water. It is perfect for a situation where you see a problem coming – like a severe weather event – or after an emergency as a way to get more water stored away while the municipal water supply is still operational. It is also great if an event is coming where you think you may lose power and your primary water source is a well. An additional bathtub full of potable water can last quite a long time.

But for true long term storage needs, there are better choices than the WaterBOB and that is to use water barrels. You can typically buy water barrels in sizes ranging from 15 gallons to 55+ gallons. They are water safe, opaque and efficient in terms of storage space. There are even heavy duty racks you can buy to stack the barrels one on top of another, allowing you to double or triple up your water space. It all depends on your budget vs available space considerations.

Large scale storage

Large scale solutions are large containers/cisterns that can hold hundreds to thousands of gallons of water. They can hold from hundreds to thousands of gallons of water and can be stored in a basement area or buried underground.

If you choose a large scale system, be sure that it is made with a food grade material as not all large scale water storage containers are made this way.

Huge scale storage

Huge scale storage systems include swimming pools and ponds in your yard. Neither of these systems is really appropriate for drinking (unless you treat the water) but they do make really good storage systems for other water uses – like flushing toilets.

I personally like having a swimming pool for just this purpose. Mind you, it will get nasty with algae (that I would filter out before using) if it sits for months without filtration and treatment but it is still good for toilets – and it can replenish itself by catching rain water.

10 HOW TO ACQUIRE WATER IN AN EMERGENCY

Storing water to last your family for a few days or even a few weeks during an emergency isn't a huge problem. Most of can find enough extra space somewhere in our house or apartment to squirrel away that amount of water (bottom of closets, under beds, etc.)

But what about for disasters that last longer than a few days or a few weeks?

Are you really going to have room to store several months to a year's worth of water? Maybe you do... but for most of us, it is unlikely. No matter how creative we get, most of us simply do not have the space to store a huge quantity of water for a potential long term emergency.

Given that this is the reality for most of us, let's examine all the ways you can acquire additional water in an emergency situation. We will look at sources that are available to just about anyone as well as many ways that are situation or environment specific.

By the end of this chapter, you will have a very robust list of water sources available to you and collection methods that will let you use these sources. By knowing which of these sources are most relevant to your situation, you will be able to make specific plans that are right for you. These plans include purchasing and storing the appropriate supplies/equipment you will need to safely use these water sources as well as dictate how much already potable water you need to save in your emergency supply.

Note that the list is presented in no particular order. Do not think the first sources listed are your best options and that you are hindered because you don't have the first source listed. Consider each water source carefully and weight it against where you live and what makes the best sense in that environment. Obviously someone who lives in the city is going to have different priority source options than someone in the lives in the country or is hiking in the woods. And someone who lives in a tropical climate is going to have very different environmental conditions than someone who lives in a climate where winter is a significant factor.

In the home

The first place to gather additional water at the start of an emergency is in the home. There are many sources available – some of which contain large sources of water. Keep in mind that all emergencies unfold in different ways. You could still have running water at the start of an emergency. But you should not assume that you will still have good water through the entire emergency. So you will want to take advantage of any time during an emergency where you have running, potable water and make sure all your storage containers are kept topped off just in case the running water supply stops working.

Let's now take a look at all the water sources you can find in your home and how you can leverage them for your survival.

- **City water** – If your property it attached to a municipal water supply, this will be a vital source of water in an emergency. Every day during an emergency, you should collect and save as much water as you can in every container you have available. This includes using your bathtub, sinks and store bought containers – including large size containers like the WaterBOB that holds a whole bathtub full of water.

  Keep in mind that for drinking water, you need to be sure the containers are food safe. But for water for other needs, like cleaning, you can use any type of clean container and for toilet flushing, you can use clean and dirty containers – including your garbage cans since that water isn't going to be used in a way that can contaminate surfaces and cause you sickness.

  The reason you want to constantly keep your containers filled when water is running is because you can never be sure when this water source will disappear – or get contaminated.

If a power down situation lasts long enough, the municipal water supply will eventually stop working. Power is needed to keep the water clean, the lines pressurized and the water flowing. If the water treatment/distribution plant loses power, you lose your water – so gather it while it is available. (Remember: it is better to have too much than not enough.) Also, if you do lose water and it is later restored, be sure there are no boil water alerts or other issues that make the water bad for drinking.

• **Well** – If you have a rural property, you are probably getting your water from a well. If you are fortunate to have a very shallow well, you can use a hand pump to extract water from it when you have no power. And if you have a well torpedo (basically a bucket on a rope), you can get water from a well of any depth as long as you have a rope long enough to get to the bottom. Or, if you have planned ahead and have an alternative power source, you could keep your well pump running.

As in the city water example above, you should pump as much water as you can store every time power goes on intermittently. Many disasters will restore power several times before it stabilizes (or goes out completely for an extended period of time) so you need to take advantage of those moments.

The best solution is to equip your house with an alternative power source – generator with plenty of food, a solar system, etc. And it would be good to wire the well pump to work with this alternative power supply. An electrician can just wire in a bypass for the house circuit breaker and supply electricity to the pump directly for a few minutes a day to get all the water you need for that day. While it costs extra, you really want to have a bypass system wired up so that you remove the relevant circuits from the grid when you are using an alternative power source for your electricity needs. If you do not do this and the grid energizes, it could cause dangerous issues with your electrical system.

In a sense, people with wells and an alternative power supply are generally better off than people with city water in a longer term disaster. The well water is more likely to be clean than city water which is working intermittently and can be subject to contamination from pressure drops in the system. Municipal water may be restored part way through a disaster but there would be boil alerts due to the pressure in the lines dropping and if you don't have power to boil the city water, it could get you sick if you drink it. Not to mention the fact that you might not get the notice about a boil water alert in a timely manner in an ongoing disaster.

• **Cold water pipes** – In a disaster when the running water stops, one of the first places you should get water is from your cold water pipes. Identify the lowest faucet in your house and turn it on with a food safe container under it to gather the water in the pipes. Keep rotating containers until the entire system is drained. Having a higher elevation faucet open will help ensure more complete drainage as it allows air to get in and the water to flow out more easily. This will not be a large supply of water but it could represent several gallons of potable water.

- **Hot water heater** – A hot water heater is actually a good storage container for water. It is clean and sanitary and generally contains between 30 and 60 gallons of water. Hot water heaters have a drain valve on the bottom that will let you get all the water out when you need it. Note that if you haven't flushed your hot water cleaner in a long time, the water could contain rust which is quite natural. You will know this is the case because the water will have a muddy brown color. The rust isn't dangerous. Just use a filter to remove it from the water.

- **Toilet tank** – The top part of the toilet holds 1-3 gallons of clean water that you can use provided you don't put bleach tablets in them to help keep the bowl fresh and clean. If you put any type of chemicals., disks, etc. in your toilet tank, do not use it for drinking water as those chemicals or their residue can be harmful. However, you do not ever want to use water in the bowl part of the toilet as it can be contaminated with bacteria.

- **Water bed** – If you have a waterbed, this is a useful source of water for flushing toilets. Since waterbed water is generally treated with a variety of chemicals, this water source is not one that you would want to drink, cook or clean with but it will give you lots of toilet flushes. A small hand pump is a great way to extract water from the water bed in small quantities for your daily flushing needs.

If you have a good water filtration system, you can convert this waterbed water into potable water but check with the filter manufacturer before you buy it to be sure it will clean out the chemicals used to keep that water "fresh" in the waterbed. Not all filtration systems will remove all the chemicals.

- **Swimming pool** – If you are lucky enough to have a swimming pool, you hit the jackpot of water storage. While you do not want to drink swimming pool water due to the chlorine and other chemicals (and biological contaminants as it sits without treatment), it is fine for flushing toilets and bathing. And with a proper treatment system, it can be used for cooking and drinking. Since the average swimming pool holds 10,000 to 20,000 gallons of water, this source will last a really long time – even with evaporation during an extended dry spell.

Another bonus of a swimming pool is that it self replenishes to a certain extent. Every rain storm will add water to your swimming pool. And if you place sloped plastic tarps around the swimming pool during a rain storm, you can direct even more water into it.

Depending on where you live and the amount of monthly rainfall, this water source could provide water for a very long time – literally years. The only disadvantage is that after a while, it will get overrun with algae. You can diminish this by stirring in pool chlorine powder from time to time and agitating the water with the cleaning brush to spread it around but eventually, the algae will win. Even then, it can still be filtered and used. Just run it through multiple layers of cheese cloth or something similar first to remove the large particles that will clog your good filter system.

- **Cistern** – If you have space, you can purchase and install a large underground cistern for water storage. Cisterns can be quite large – up to several thousand gallons in size – and make for a great backup water supply. This is an item you would need to purchase in advance of a disaster though. If you have the space and money, consider it like you would an insurance policy. You may never need it but you will be glad you have it in an emergency.

There are many ways to tie a cistern into your home water system – from having the cistern between your water supply (well/city water) and your house to having one elevated from your house to provide you gravity fed water so that you have running water even when there is no power to run a well pump. Talk to your installer to discuss options that work for your particular needs.

- **Water treatment system** – Many people – especially people with wells - use water treatment systems. Usually they are installed to soften the water (i.e. remove the high iron content) to help your plumbing system have a longer life.

Depending on the water treatment system installed at your house, it could be holding hundreds of gallons of water, or none. It all depends on its configuration and what is treatments is is applying to your incoming water source. For instance, at one property we had, the water had a high sulfur content and we had a 300 gallon tank with a sprayer on top. The sprayer would allow the sulfur gas to evaporate from the water and then the system pulled from that tank to supply the house. When power went out, it represented a 300 gallon supply of drinking water for us. But at another house, we just had a system that removed iron. It held about 3-5 gallons in a flush tank that was too salty to be used.

- **In line water tanks** – You can purchase tanks that you put in line with your plumbing system – just like your hot water heater. these tanks can hold anywhere from 50 to hundreds of gallons of water. While it does take advance planning and space to use these tanks, it is an option for holding hundreds to thousands of gallons of water for emergencies.

  In line tanks are a great option for houses that have a basement or crawl space under the house where the units can be installed without having an impact on your living area. They are not really a good option for houses with a slab floor as you typically find in South Florida and similar areas where houses are built on slabs rather than on foundations.

- **Freezer** – Most people have either ice cube trays or an ice maker in their freezer. And some people have manual defrost freezers – especially in RVs. This ice in the freezer can represent a source of water. However you want to leave it in the freezer as long as possible if there is a power outage to help keep the food there frozen. A good freezer can keep the food cold up to a day or more depending on its design and how tightly it is packed – but you should have a plan to use that food if the power is going to be out a while or be prepared to dispose of it. Once the ice no longer holds value for keeping the food frozen, it can be used for drinking water.

- **Canned goods** – Canned goods are often foods packaged in liquid. Most of us just throw away the liquid in that can of peas when we cook it but it is drinkable. It might not taste as delicious as pure water but it is a source of water when you don't have other sources. As a bonus, all canned goods are pre-cooked so you can eat the food right out of the can. That gives you two for one – a bit of water to drink and food you can eat without heating – saving both your stored water supply and your heating fuel.

- **Dehumidifier** – If you have a source of electricity (generator, solar, etc.), you can run a dehumidifier. A dehumidifier is basically a box that removes water from the air and stores it in a container. Larger units can pull out several gallons a day in a fairly humid environment.

  Even if you are in a situation where your power is off (or running intermittently), keep your humidifier on. When you get power restored, even for a short time, it will generate some water for you. And if power is on for a while, keep draining the tank and saving it until you are certain things have stabilized for your situation.

Natural water sources

Natural water sources can provide you with an abundance of water. While not as convenient as water pumped right into your house, natural supplies can keep you well stocked. Just be sure to take proper safety precautions before drinking from any natural source.

- **Rain** — Rain is an interesting water source because so much can be done to replenish your water supply if you are   prepared.

  The obvious first thing you can do as a prepper is to live in an area that has abundant annual rainfall. (In case you are thinking of moving, http://www.usclimatedata.com/ is a great research website. It gives rainfall data for every significant   city   in   the   United   States.

  Obviously, if you live in a desert environment, rain water is going is a poor natural water source for you. But if you live in a rainy environment, rain can supply all your water needs if you have the means to collect and store it.

  Let's look at the many ways you can collect and use rainwater.

  1. Collect   rain   that   lands   on   your   roof.

     During a rainstorm, a tremendous amount of water lands on your roof. To give you an idea how much, you can collect up to 600 gallons for every 1,000 sqft of roof space you have assuming a rain storm that drops one inch of rain. So if you have 2,000 sqft of roof space and get 20 inches of rain a year, you can theoretically collect a whopping 24,000 gallons   of   water   a   year.

     Please note that rainwater collected this way will be dirty as it will have whatever dirt, dust, grime and contaminants were on the roof at the time it rains mixed in with it. This will all need to be filtered out if you use this as a source of drinking water.

There is only one effective way to collect rainwater from your roof. You need to have gutters installed and some sort of system to catch the rainfall — barrels or holding tanks — or even a pipe system to transport the water into a large holding tank. Obviously all this takes a bit of advance planning to be useful.

And unfortunately you do need to check your community's rules regarding rainwater. Some communities have decided that you do not own that water that falls on your roof and it is actually illegal for you to collect it. Just one more thing to check if you are planning to move to a new location.

We're fortunate to live in a very enlightened area with respect to roof runoff. The local government will even sell you subsidized rain barrels. Mind you, the subsidy is off of the full retail price which means you can find other sources for the same price or even a little less. But at least they are advertising the idea and will help you set up a system. Much nicer than a town that fines you for collecting your own water.

2. You can funnel clean rainwater landing on your yard into storage tanks — or even containers like

kiddie swimming pools. The amount you can gather really depends on how your land is laid out.

The process to collect rainwater this way is simple. You just lay out plastic sheeting on an incline and have your holding container at the bottom of the incline. Much of the rain that falls on the plastic sheeting will flow into your container(s). And if you have a flat piece of land, you can always dig a small "pond" and cover it with plastic to catch rain water.

3. The worst case scenario of rain water collection is to just put all the wide mouth containers, buckets and towels you can find out in the rain. As they fill (or in the case of the towels; get soaked), transfer the contents to another storage container and put them back outside. Keep repeating this during the entire rain storm and you will get some water. To increase your yield, you can stick funnels into the opening of containers to increase the collection area.

    The whole point here is that if you are in an emergency situation, rain can be a significant water replacement source for you and your family. Figure out what rain capture methods work for your situation and be sure you stock the supplies you need to take advantage of this source.

*   **Snow/ice** - Like rain, snow & ice can be a great source of water in winter climates. It is easy to collect and bring inside to melt it and then top off your storage containers.

And the best part of snow/ice is that in a cold climate, it can stick around for weeks – letting your collect at a relaxed pace. This is actually an advantage over rain – which is gone once the storm stops.

Like all other natural water sources, you should purify it before drinking. You can never be sure what you might scoop up when collecting the snow.

- **A pond on your property** – If you are fortunate enough to have a small pond on your property or have a lakefront property or have a neighbor with a pond who is willing to share, you will have a great source of water available to you in any disaster.

If you don't have a pond on your property but have the space for one and the money to get one dug (and zoning allows), you can put one on your property. If your water table is high enough or if it rains enough, your pond will almost always have water in it. And if not, you could set up a solar powered well to keep it filled. When the sun shines, the pump runs and pulls water from the well into the pond – keeping it topped off. This is of course an expensive solution but it is one that may work for you.

Also, don't discount your neighbor down the street who has a pond. They may be amenable to you taking water from time to time. Even if all you can get it enough to flush your toilets a few times a day, that represents a huge savings of your own water supply – and helps keep things much more sanitary.

- **Rivers/Streams/Creeks, etc.** – Near our house, we have a creek that runs all year long. The flow does get a bit low during dry spells but it never stops flowing.

  If you have one of these supplies on your property or nearby, it can provide all the water you need – provided neighbors don't mind you going on their property to collect   water.

  Depending on zoning and government environmental regulations, you may also be able to set up a small dam in a stream running on your property. This gives you two things. It gives you a pond that will always stay full if the stream always runs. And you may be able to set up a generation system with the dam to generate enough electricity for your needs. (And you can stock the pond with fish for a ready food source.)

- **Know your surface water table depth** – Did you know that in many places you can dig a very shallow well and collect water from it. While the task can be backbreaking to do with a shovel, if you have a water table that is only a few feet deep, it might be worth the effort to dig a hole that deep and let it naturally fill with water from the surrounding   ground.

  In South Florida, where I lived for many years, we had a pond that was groundwater filled in this way. The top of the water level in the pond was only a few feet below the surface level of the land because in South Florida, the surface water table is literally only a few feet below ground. If we didn't have a pond and needed water, it would have been no problem digging a makeshift well to get water to meet our needs.

You will need to dig the well to a few feet below the top of the water level. So if your water table starts at five feet below ground, you would want to dig your well at least 7-8 feet deep. This will keep water in the well as the water level fluctuates and is deep enough to fully immerse a bucket to extract a full compliment of water.

Extreme Water Sources

Extreme water sources are all the odd places you can find water in the wild. Most will only provide small amounts of water but knowing these sources could mean the difference between life and death – especially if you find yourself stranded in the wild.

- **Water garden** – There are a variety of plants you could grow in your yard that are water sources. (Or you might find them in a neighbor's yard or growing in the wild if you find yourself stranded away from home.) Good water plants are bamboo, banana plants, cacti, coconut palms and water vines. They are each good sources of water and should be planted if they grow in your environment and will fit into your landscaping. Here are more details on each of these plants.

  1. Bamboo - Bamboo is a fascinating grass. (Yes, as amazing as it sounds, bamboo really is a grass.) Bamboo grows in segments – with each segment having a hollow center. If you cut a piece of bamboo between two joints, you will often find

that this hollow space is full of clean water.

You can tell if bamboo has water in it by either shaking the plant and listening or tapping a segment and listening for a dull sound – rather than a loud, sharp sound which would indicate an empty   segment.

To collect the water, just cut a notch right above a joint and let the water drain into a container. You can drink the water as is. It is clean and potable.

Bamboo is also useful for making water carrying devices. Just cut out a segment by cutting just below the bottom joint and just above the top joint. You can then carve a hole in the top joint and two holes in the side of the segment near the top to run a thin rope through for a carrying strap. This will give you a nice carrying tube for a water supply. Depending on the size of the particular piece of, it can be a very large container – holding a quart or more of water.

2. Banana Plants - In addition to producing delicious fruit, bananas are a great source of water. But you need to do some work to get at the water source.

    Here is what you need to do to collect water from banana trees. First, you need to cut the banana plant about three inches above the ground, removing everything above it. Then hollow out the center of the stump you just created – making a bowl   shaped   depression.

This depression will fill with water drawn up from the root system. Let it fill completely and then drain it. You should not drink this first bit of water. Once you remove the water, wait for it to fill up again. This second (and subsequent) filling will be clean   drinking   water.

Because the root system stays alive, the bowl will keep replenishing itself making it a good long term source of water if planted outdoors. This means that if you have access to several banana plants, you can build a fairly robust water source from them.

3. Cacti - Cacti are big water storage plants. They are designed to live in a harsh, unforgiving environment and have evolved with thick skins that protect the water which is contained in the sponge like pulp in its center. This water can be collected. It is quite a bit of work and you need to be careful of the sharp spines covering the cactus.

Here are the steps you need to follow.

First, you need to work with a fairly large plant to extract a reasonable water supply. Small cacti are not worth the effort. You need to cut the top off of the plant and scoop out the pulp. Place the pulp in a cotton shirt or cloth and squeeze the water out of it directly into your mouth or in a container. Do not eat the pulp.

4. Coconut Palms - Coconut palms are famous for coconuts. As anyone who has bought a coconut in the store knows, it is full of coconut water.

   Each coconut can supply a cup or more of coconut water. When the coconut is green, this water is highly nutritious – and in fact you should eat the pulp against the shell too. It has an odd gelatinous texture when it is green but is quite nutritious.

   As the coconut ages and dries out, the character of the water changes. It develops an oil that can cause diarrhea so you should not drink old coconut water in large quantities.

5. Water vines - Water vines are a great source of water. Water vines tend to be one to six inches thick at the ground and thin out as they grow up the sides of trees.

   There are many types of water vines and not all of them produce usable water. If you cut one and it has white sap or milky liquid or tastes sour or bitter, it is not a source of water. However if it produces a clear fluid with a woody or sweet taste, it is a good source of water. It is worth the time to get to know what water vines in your area are good water sources as part of your prepper education.

   To harvest the water in a water vine, you will make

an initial cut at the top of the vine (as high up as you can reach) and then a 2nd cut at the bottom of the vine. Allow the liquid to drain into a container and drink it as is. If you have no container and choose to drink directly from the vine, avoid contact with the vine as the outer layers could contain irritants.

- **Rocks** - Rocks are great repositories of water. Many rocks have imperfections – holes or depressions – where water can accumulate. And larger ones can have large fissures where bigger pools of water can accumulate and be available for many days or even weeks after a rainstorm. For a fissure, you will probably need a hose to siphon out water unless it is large enough to allow you to lower a container into it.

- **Condensation** – Condensation and dew are sources of water created by changes in temperature that condense water out of the air. You are familiar with dew as the wetness on your grass in the morning. This can be collected with absorbent towels and then squeezed into containers. When wiping water off the ground, it is probably dirty and it would be best to filter it before drinking.

Another option to collect dew is to lay a sheet of plastic over a hole in the ground and weight its center down with a rock. Place a container below the that center point and the condensation that accumulates on the plastic will drip into the container. The amount of water you can collect depends on how moist the air is, the change in temperature that occurs and the area you are collecting.

Neither method will generate a huge quantity of water but when you are in a survival situation, the more ways you can collect water, the more secure you will be.

- **Animal trails** – If you can identify an animal trail, it could lead to a water source. It could take a while to follow it to a source but generally well traveled animal paths are well traveled because they do lead to water.

- **Birds** – If you notice a large number of birds congregating in a specific area, there is generally a water source nearby. Birds spend a lot of time washing in even small water sources so chances are this will lead you to a dirty water source that must be filtered before drinking.

- **Dry river bed** – If you stumble upon a dry river bed, do not assume that it is a bust. It could lead you to a water bonanza. Find a low point in the river bed and start digging. Often there is water just inches to a foot or so below the surface.

- **Sea water** – You should not drink salt water. It will do more harm than good. However, if you have a method of distilling it to remove the salt, it can be made potable. This is actually a simple process that can be done with sunlight, some plastic and a collection device. You are basically evaporating the water with sunlight, condensing it on the plastic and capturing it in your collection container.

- **Vegetation water still** – A plant water still is basically a still that is extracting water from plant matter using sunlight. It is a pretty simple process and if you can set up several, you can collect enough water for survival. It works with living plant matter — like nonpoisonous tree branches. Here   are   the   steps:

1.   Find a plant or tree with a lot of leaves that you can reach that also gets lots of direct sunlight.

2.   Enclose the leaves with a bag and put a rock in the bag.

3.   Close the bag securely — making sure the rock forms a "V" at the bottom of the bag. (This is where the water will be collected.)

4.   Let the still work for 24 hours and collect your water.

5. Repeat on another part of the plant for the next day.

There are many other ways to gather water but this list will certainly give you a good start in keeping yourself alive and possibly even thriving in an extended emergency situation.

One final note and reminder

Not all liquids are beneficial. Three liquids you should never drink are urine, sea water and blood. All three of these liquids will speed up dehydration.

11 WATER CONSERVATION AND RATIONING

Water conservation is simply the act of using less water to accomplish the same activities and is a good skill to master. Since water could potentially be scarce in an emergency situation, it is good to know the various ways you can save the water you are using in your day to day tasks. By taking steps now to make water conservation a habit, you automatically be using less water when an emergency arises. (And if you are on city water, you will be pleasantly surprised by the reduction in your monthly water bill.)

The next several pages examine typical uses of water in your house and how you can use less or even no water in each of these activities. And we will follow that with a discussion of what to do when drinkable water supplies get low and the end of the emergency still looks a long way off.

Conservation

When water is available – as it typically is every day in your home – I believe you should make choices that are right for you and your family. For instance, some people love long showers while others feel they are wasteful. I figure that if you are not living in a drought condition, it is your decision how much water you choose to use for your daily activities.

However, understanding ways to conserve water can benefit you in an emergency. Emergencies can be weather or geological events which can cause a full loss of your standard water supply. Or they can be something more mild like the severe water usage restrictions imposed in California in 2015 to stretch water supplies during their multi-year severe drought. They used government penalties as the stick to get people to conserve water supplies and it worked surprising well, with most municipalities reaching or very nearly reaching their targeted water use reductions.

Let's examine many your home water uses and what steps you can take to reduce usage at each of these points.

- **Toilet** – Depending on the age of your toilet, it may be using a small amount of water or a large amount. Most modern toilets are water efficient. Most older ones are water hogs. The modern generation of water efficient toilets use just 1.6 gallons per flush and super high efficiency toilets that just just 1.28 gallons per flush while older toilets (and first generation water efficient toilets) are much more greedy – using up to seven gallons per flush (or over multiple flushes in the old style efficient toilets.)

There are several things you can do to reduce water usage in a toilet – even a modern water efficient toilet.

1. Flush the toilet only when necessary, rather than after every use. If you can go from 10-15 flushes a day to just 2-3, the water savings really build up.

2. Purchase a new set of toilet components that allow you to do a low water flush for urine and a full flush for everything else. Basically these work by flushing a smaller amount of water for liquid waste than for solid waste. This works because it is easier to get the flushing action when there are no solid waste in the toilet – thus requiring less water to cause a flush to occur.

3. Place a brick, water bottle filled with sand or rocks or similar heavy object in your toilet tank to reduce the amount of water it takes to fill the tank to the "full" line. After you add the object, be sure to do several test flushes. You need to be sure you did not reduce the available water in the tank so much that it no longer flushes properly. Also take care in the placement of the object to be sure it doesn't interfere with the movement of any of the internal parts.

4. Purchase a new water efficient toilet. These will use the minimum amount of water necessary for an effective flush and often have the components

to do urine flushes and full flushes. Plus, many communities offer rebates for replacing old toilets for new, water efficient units. So if your unit is looking tired, check with your local government to see if you can wrangle a discount for your upgrade.

- **Shower** – A standard shower uses about 2.5 gallons of water a minute. If you have a low flow shower head, it will use two gallons or less per minute.

There are two ways you can reduce water usage when taking a shower. The first is to simply take shorter showers. The second is to put a flow reducer in the shower head to reduce the amount of water that flows through the shower head every minute. When you use a flow reducer, it could compromise the shower experience for you so you may need to shop a few different flow reducer/shower head combinations to find a solution that gives you a satisfactory experience.

There is a third option but it involves a fairly large cost. That option is to re-plumb your house to put in an inline on demand water heater unit close to the shower. An inline unit will give you almost instant hot water so you don't need to wait as long before hot water starts coming out. I know that in our house, we need to wait at least a minute (longer in winter) before the shower water is hot. And over time that wastes a lot of water. While it is a chore, you could actually put a bucket in your shower to capture that "too cold to enter" water to use for a "free" toilet flush or for watering your garden.

And if you are thinking of doing any plumbing work, you can have the plumber a "gray water" line system to capture shower/bath/sink type water in a holding tank. This water can be used for watering your lawn and other outdoor water uses. But before taking a step like this, be sure it doesn't violate any zoning laws in your area. Many towns do not allow "gray water" lines in houses.

- **Baths** – Baths use a lot of water. A typical bathtub will hold 35 to 50 gallons of water. And larger jacuzzi style bathtubs can hold much more water.

But once the bath is over, that water can be reused.

For instance, you can scoop the water out and use it to flush the toilet by pouring a bucket of the water into the toilet bowl. You can also use it to hand wash some clothes or to water plants, give your pets a bath, etc.

Many of these additional activities will leave the tub dirty and will require it to be cleaned before you take your next bath so if you are doing one of these activities, it is a good idea to set aside a bucket of water for cleaning the tub before repurposing the remaining water for washing your clothes, etc.

- **Dishwasher** – Modern dishwashers are very water efficient so if you have an old one that dies, you will find yourself using much less water after replacing the machine with a modern one.

Aside from replacement, the only thing you can really do

to reduce water usage with a dishwasher is to make sure it is full before running it. Running a ½ full dishwasher uses just as much water as a full one so it is better to wait until you have it completely full. Or if you don't use many dishes throughout the day, it may be more water efficient to wash them by hand.

- **Washing Machine** – Modern washing machines are generally water efficient. For instance, the one we have even automatically calculates how big the load of clothes is and calculates how much water it needs to add automatically. That means there is no more mistakenly forgetting to twist the dial from full load to light load to save water. It is done automatically.

Assuming you have an older machine, the only thing you can do to reduce water consumption is to be sure the fill dial is set to reflect the load size. (You can also choose to wear certain garments more times before washing them to cut down on the number of loads a month but that is not always appealing.)

- **Kitchen Sink** – The kitchen sink is like a mini tub. You can fill it with water and use that tub to do things – like wash dishes. If you have a dual sink, this is very efficient. You wash the dishes in the sink that is filled with water and place the cleaned dishes in the empty sink. When you are done, you rinse all the clean dishes in running water to remove all the soap residue, etc. If you only have a single sink setup, you can use a plastic tub to hold the dishes before rinsing them.

The way you can waste great quantities of water with any sink is to just leave the water constantly running while you are doing your cleaning activity. Turn it off when not directly using the water and you will save quite a bit.

Also remember that you can repurpose sink water when you are done for watering your yard. You probably wouldn't want to use it for other activities as it is likely pretty dirty – much more so than bath water as an example.

- **Bathroom Sink** – Like the kitchen sink, the bathroom sink can be very efficiently used if you turn off the water when not directly using it. Many people turn it on and leave it on while shaving, washing their face or brushing their teeth. This is very wasteful and represents a good area for savings.

- **Water For Cooking** – If you are cooking pasta or another food that has lots of leftover water, you can reuse this water in your yard or garden. The exception is if you are boiling meat. You do not want to pour all the fat into the garden.

You can also be careful of the amount of water you use when cooking. Many times we add more water than we need to a pot. For instance, pasta boxes often tell you to boil four to six quarts of water to cook properly. Use the lower end and over time, the savings can add up. And if you are in a water rationing situation, you can actually cook your pasta in much less water – but you have to watch it and stir it more often to be sure it cooks properly and doesn't run out of water.

- **Fix All Water Leaks** – It goes without saying that plumbing leaks can waste huge amounts of water. We've all seen the news stories of people getting water bills for 25,000 gallons of water use in a single month. Sometimes, these bills are from meters malfunctioning but most of the time they represent a leak somewhere in your plumbing.

  Leaks can occur in toilets and all faucets. These should always be fixed as soon as possible as they can waste a huge amount of water over time. For toilets, you will know if the tank is leaking as you will hear it fill frequently when it hasn't been flushed.

  It is also possible for your water pipes to leak – and this may be unnoticed, especially if it is an underground pipe that is leaking. But you could have visible links – like the plumbing under your sink.

  If you are on metered water, it is pretty easy to tell if you have a leak. You can just watch the meter for a few minutes when no one is using water in the house. If it doesn't change, you have no leaks.

  If you have a well, it is a bit harder to notice leaks in buried pipes. About the only way you can guess is if you see a particularly green or wet spot somewhere along the path where the pipe runs from the well into your house. Or you may notice the well pump cycling on and off regularly when no one is using water in the house.

- **Use Outdoor Hoses Efficiently** – Make sure your hoses are attached tightly so they do not leak water at the connection and use a nozzle so you can direct the water only where and when you need it.

  Also, if your hose does spring a leak, you can buy hose repair kits to patch the leak or cut off the bad section of hose. For a few dollars, you can probably save 49 feet of that 50 dollar hose.

- **Outdoor Cleaning** – Most people like to keep their car and house clean. This means washing the car as needed and pressure washing your siding, sidewalks and driveways. About the only way to save water here (aside from not cleaning) is to be sure the water is only on while you actually need it and that the hoses are not leaking.

- **Watering Your Lawn/Garden** – If you want to keep a nice lawn or if you have a garden, you are going to need to water from time to time to keep everything looking good and health.

  For lawns, you should only water early in the morning or late at night to give the lawn time to absorb the water before the sun evaporates it away. Also water only a few times a week. Watering daily is not necessary and you can even end up overwatering your lawn.

  For gardens, the best solution is a drip irrigation system which delivers water directly to each plant without waste. Also, putting mulch around the plants will retain water longer – reducing the number of times you need to water.

This list is not comprehensive but it does touch on the major water uses in a typical household. I'm sure that if you think a bit, you can come up with other areas where you use water and ways you can conserve water in those areas.

Rationing

Rationing of water is a very situation specific issue. You may be forced to make very different choices based on where you are located and what water resources you have available to you.

Let's look at some of the issues you must consider when deciding how to ration water in a shortage situation.

First, let's look at the biology. It is a simple truth that if you restrict your daily water consumption, you will become progressively weaker and less able to function (i.e. you will become dehydrated.) Dehydration during rationing is such a dangerous situation that most survivalists recommend that you drink water rather than save it when you are in an emergency situation. This is based on the assumption that you will stand a better chance of finding a new water source or rescue if you are not suffering debilitating dehydration.

However, most of us will not be lost in the woods in a disaster situation. We will hopefully be at our homes (or be able to get to them) where we have a water cache. And hopefully we will have identified sources of natural water that we can also collect to supplement our stored supply – to put off the need to ration water.

In this survival situation, you can afford to drink a bit less every day as you are probably not in a true life or death survival situation. It might be hugely inconvenient and you may need to make choices you wouldn't normally make to stretch your supplies but in most instances, things will be fixed, supplies will be made available and things will improve.

The key question in this case is – how long? How long will it take for things to get back to normal? How long until supplies start being available again?

You need to answer these questions to make proper decisions on how to use your supplies. Short of a complete and unfixable breakdown of society, having a year supply of food and water for your family should get you through almost any disaster in really good shape.

Why do I say this? Just look at any first world country disaster and what do you see? You see folks from unaffected regions of the world pouring in to the area to help out. They bring in supplies and labor to dig out and help rebuild the affected community. You also see people choosing to leave their community to go to an unaffected area so they do not need to endure the hardships of rebuilding. In other words, short of a complete breakdown of society, mobility generally exists.

Even poorer countries see great outpouring of aid. When Haiti was destroyed in 2010, many other countries pitched in and helped them recover. (Unfortunately, that process is still continuing and lots of aid never seemed to make it to the people but that is another story.) The point is that short of a worldwide catastrophe, those outside the disaster area deliver aid to those who are afflicted. That means that if you can hold out where you are for a month or longer waiting on assistance, you are in great shape for almost any disaster that could happen.

12 WATER AND SANITATION

Water is a cornerstone of keeping our lives sanitary. It allows us to clean ourselves and our surroundings, removes waste from our house and gives us the sanitary conditions that keep us from getting sick.

However when water supplies are low, compromises and alternatives need to be examined to handle these useful (and often essential) functions. This chapter will examine the various issues regarding sanitation and discuss options to deal with them in a low water situation.

Sanitation

Sanitation (cleanliness) is important at all times – and especially in hard times. It helps prevent the spread of disease. Something as simple as washing your hands when preparing food can prevent your family from getting sick.

But in times of water scarcity, basic sanitation and hygiene may be neglected in an effort to stretch limited supplies of water. Or worse, neglected because of the inconvenience of not having running water (even though you have plenty in your water storage program.)

This section examines several hygiene related issues and proposes alternative solutions that you can practice to keep you and your family safe while conserving your precious water supply.

Human Waste

We tend not to think about what happens when we flush the toilet but in some situations, it is forced on us. Usually it is just a clogged toilet but it can be a much more serious problem that causes a large amount of sewage to flow into your house.

There are two common waste disposal methods:

- city sewer system

- septic tank

A sewer system consists of underground pipes and a series of pump stations that move the waste from your house to a treatment center for processing.

A septic tank system uses gravity to flow the waste into a large tank buried on your property where it basically composts and a leach field where the liquid wastes break down. Periodically, you need to have a septic tank pumped out to keep the waste from backing up into your house – which will happen if it is full.

In emergency situations, either of these two systems can fail and interestingly, the septic system is the more robust of the two as it does not depend on pumps to migrate the waste away from your house/neighborhood.

Sewer systems can back up when the power is down for too long. When things are working properly, the waste flows through the pipes to pumping substations which move it down the line to the next pumping station and so on until it finally gets to its end destination – the processing center. If power is down for an extended period of time and people keep flushing their toilets, the waste will back up into the pipes and can actually build up enough pressure to flow into your house – creating an unsanitary mess. This is made worse if there is also flooding which can increase the volume and pressure in the pipes if the flood waters find their way into the sewer system.

In a septic tank system, the only danger you face in an emergency is if you have a flood covering your yard. If the flood waters stay long enough, it can cause a backflow into your house.

[Keep in mind that during any flood situation, all water should be considered suspect. City water can get contaminated as can your well and any surface water sources that have been exposed to flood water. Take extra safety measures when using water during a flood and for a period of time afterwords. And if you have a well, you should probably perform a basic water quality test if the flood waters could have contaminated it.]

Fortunately, there is a way to stop backflow of sewage into your house from happening. You can have a plumber install a backflow valve in your sewage line. This will prevent backflow if the septic tank or sewage system becomes compromised. It is a small investment that is worth making. It is important to note that a backflow valve will only prevent entry of sewage from outside your house. It will not prevent toilets from overflowing if the flushes have nowhere to go because of pressure external to the backflow valve stopping the waste from getting into the sewer/septic system.

Of course, using a toilet in a survival situation also assumes that you have the water to flush it. If you do not, there are several options for safely disposing of human waste. In no particular order, they are:

- Composting toilet. Although expensive, a composting toilet is a self contained toilet system that actually composts the toilet waste. It holds quite a bit of waste and when it gets full, you just empty it out. There are several different types of composting toilets so if you go with this waste option, be sure to study the various products and choose the best one for your situation and needs.

- Outhouse. Outhouses have worked well as toilets for millenia. They are really nothing more than a deep hole in the ground with a stand and toilet seat cover over them for you to take care of your business. They are an excellent solution and are something you can create yourself with little more than a bit of hard labor and some wood to build a bit of privacy. The only caution is that you want to build your outhouse far away from your well or other water source on your property to ensure that there is no contamination of that water supply.

If you choose to build an outhouse – or think you might in the future – there are plenty of illustrated tutorials available on the internet. Just type "how to build an outhouse" in your favorite search engine.

- Potty Bucket – A very inexpensive solution is a potty bucket with liners and chemicals to treat the waste. They are very efficient and a good choice for an emergency toilet. When the bucket gets full, just top up with treatment chemicals, tie the liner and dispose of it in a hole – again far away from any possible water source.

Hand/Body Cleanliness

The next aspect of cleanliness to explore is keeping your body clean. Unless you have running water – or a good supply of extra water like a swimming pool – you probably won't be able to take too many baths or showers. Even washing your hands could be a luxury if you are running low on stockpiled water.

Fortunately, there are many solutions – some very old and some relatively new.

- Sanitary gel is a gel based product that you can use to wash your hands. Just put a squirt on your hands and rub them together. The gel evaporates and your hands are pretty much germ free. And it has a very long shelf life so it is something you can add to your preparedness supplies.

If you are thinking of using sanitary gel, you should test different brands before stocking up. Some brands may cause your hands to dry out and some leave residues that could sting your eyes if you rub them soon after using the gel.

- Baby wipes – These pre-moistened towelettes can be used to clean you all over. They are made gentle so that they can be used to clean a baby's delicate skin so you can use them pretty much anywhere on your body without risk of rashes, etc. And like all alternative products, you should test out brands to see which brand works best for you.

- Sponge bath – You can do a good job cleaning yourself with a sponge and/or a few cloths. It does use water but a gallon of water can clean you pretty completely.

- Rainstorm/Swimming Pool/Stream – As a last resort type of measure, you can always go out in a rainstorm with a bar of soap and clean yourself it the rain isn't too cold. Or use a swimming pool or other outdoor source of water.

Washing clothes

Just like washing yourself, washing clothes needs to be done in a water friendly manner. This means hand washing in a small tub or if you happen to have a stream or river on your property, you can wash them in the running water. You can always use "gently used" water for this process to extend the life of your sources. For instance, after a sponge bath, use that water to wash some of your clothes.

Chances are good that you will not get your clothes as

clean by this method as using a washing machine but remember that in an emergency, your goal is to limit the amount of water you use. Looking spotless is nice but being sanitary is really the goal here.

Disposing of garbage

Like it or not, there will still be garbage generated post disaster. All those cans of food waste, paper waste, etc. need to go somewhere far away from where you live to be sure you are not attracting unwanted pests.

The best way to dispose of this waste is to dig a pit and bury it or burn it. But if you decide to burn it, be sure you are not burning anything that will make a poisonous or noxious gas. That means you do not want to burn plastics, batteries, household chemical bottles and similar items.

And like an outhouse, you want your garbage dump to be far away from your water source if you have a well or are lucky enough to have a stream or other running water source on your property.

Well Disinfection

If you are fortunate enough to have a well on your property and a means to extract water from it post disaster, you may find it advantageous to disinfect it — especially if the disaster was flood related.

Disinfecting a well is a relatively simple process and only needs pure bleach with no additives. From the CDC, here is the procedure:

Safety Precautions before starting

Clear hazards away from wells before cleaning and disinfecting wells after floods and other natural disasters.

Follow these precautions:

- Turn off all electricity to the well area before working with it.

- Carefully inspect the area around the well for hazards such as power lines on the ground or in the water; sharp metal, glass, or wood debris; open holes; and slippery conditions.

- Do not enter the well pit. Gases and vapors can build up in well pits, creating a hazardous environment. Clear debris from dug wells using buckets, grappling hooks, nets, and long-handled scoops.

- Before the power is turned back on, a qualified electrician, well contractor, or pump contractor may need to check the equipment wiring system.

- Use rubber gloves and wear protective goggles or a face shield and a protective apron when working with chlorine solutions.

- When mixing and handling chlorine solutions, work in well-ventilated areas and avoid breathing vapors.

- Warn users not to drink or bathe in water until all the well disinfection steps have been completed and the well has been thoroughly flushed and testing indicates it is safe to use.

Disinfection Procedure for Bored or Dug Wells

Bored and dug wells can be difficult to disinfect because the shallow depth and inadequate protection can allow contaminants to enter the well.

Follow these steps to disinfect bored or dug wells:

1. If the well is equipped with an electrical pump, turn off all electricity and clear debris from around the top of the well.

2. Repair the electrical system and pump if needed. Contact a qualified electrician, well contractor, or pump contractor if you are not experienced with this type of work.

3. Start the pump and run water until it is clear. Use the outside faucet nearest to the well to drain the potentially contaminated water from the well and keep the unsafe well water out of the interior household plumbing. If no pump is installed, bail water from the well with a bucket until water is clear.

4. If the well is connected to interior home plumbing, close valves to any water softener unit.

Use the below table to determine the amount of liquid household bleach (5%-6%) needed to disinfect the well. Use only unscented bleach.

Table 1. Approximate Amount of Bleach for Disinfection of a Bored or Dug Well

Depth of Water	Diameter of Well					
	½ foot	1 foot	2 feet	3 feet	4 feet	5 feet
10 feet	½ cup	1 ¾ cups	7 cups	1 gal	1 ¾ gal	2 ¾ gal
20 feet	1 cup	3.5 cups	14 cups	2 gal	3 ½ gal	5 ½ gal
30 feet	1.5 cups	5 ¼ cups	1 ¼ gal	3 gal	5 ¼ gal	8 ¼ gal
40 feet	2 cups	7 cups	1 ¾ gal	4 gal	7 gal	11 gal
50 feet	2.5 cups	8 ¾ cups	2 ¼ gal	5 gal	8 ¾ gal	13 ¾ gal

Notes:

- Use only unscented household liquid chlorine bleach.

- Bleach concentrations can vary between 5% and 6%.

- Quantities given in this table are approximate and are rounded to the nearest practical measurement. Amounts given are calculated in accordance with reaching a chlorine concentration of 100 mg/L

Key:

gal: gallon

1 cup = 8 fluid ounces

1 gallon = 16 cups

Using a 5-gallon bucket, mix the bleach from Table 1

with 3-5 gallons of water (12-19 liters).

Add the bleach water mixture to the well. Avoid all electrical connections. Attach a clean hose to an outside faucet and use it to circulate water back into the well for thorough mixing. If no pump is installed, mix water by pouring it back into the well using a bucket.

Rinse the inside of the well casing with a garden hose or bucket for 5-10 minutes.

Open all faucets inside the home and run the water until you notice a strong odor of chlorine (bleach) at each faucet. Turn off all faucets and allow the solution to remain in the well and plumbing for at least 12 hours.

After at least 12 hours, attach a hose to an outside faucet and drain the chlorinated water onto a non-vegetated area such as a driveway. Continue draining until the chlorine odor disappears. Avoid draining into open sources of water (streams, ponds, etc.).

Turn on all indoor faucets and run water until the chlorine odor disappears.

Until well water has been tested, boil it (roiling boil for 1 minute) before use or utilize an alternative water source. Wait at least 7-10 days after disinfection, then have the water in your well sampled. Water sampling cannot be done until all traces of chlorine have been flushed from the system.

Disinfection Procedure for Drilled or Driven Wells

Follow these steps:

If the well is equipped with an electrical pump, turn off all electricity and clear debris from around the top of the well.

Repair the electrical system and pump if needed. Contact a qualified electrician, well contractor, or pump contractor if you are not experienced with this type of work.

Start the pump and run water until it is clear. Use the outside faucet nearest to the well to drain the potentially contaminated water from the well and keep the unsafe well water out of the interior household plumbing. If no pump is installed, bail water from the well with a bucket or other device until the water is clear.

If the well is connected to interior home plumbing, close valves to any water softener units.

Use Table 2 to determine the amount of liquid household bleach (5%-6%) needed to disinfect the well. Use only unscented bleach. For a table in metric units, please see Table 2.1: Approximate Amount of Bleach for Disinfection of a Drilled or Driven Well (Metric).

Table 2. Approximate Amount of Bleach for Disinfection of a Drilled or Driven Well

Dept	Diameter of Well

h of Water	2 inch	4 inch	6 inch	8 inch	10 inch	24 inch
10 feet	¾ tbsp	3 ¼ tbsp	½ cup	¾ cup	1 ¼ cups	7 cups
20 feet	1 ½ tbsp	6 ½ tbsp	1 cup	1 ½ cups	2 ½ cups	14 cups
30 feet	2 ¼ tbsp	9 ¾ tbsp	1 ½ cups	2 ¼ cups	3 ¾ cups	1 ¼ gal
40 feet	3 tbsp	13 tbsp	2 cups	3 cups	5 cups	1 ¾ gal
50 feet	3 ¾ tbsp	1 cup	2 ½ cups	3 ¾ cups	6 ¼ cups	2 ¼ gal
100 feet	7 ½ tbsp	2 cups	5 cups	7 ½ cups	12 ½ cups	4 ½ gal

Notes:

- Use only unscented household liquid chlorine bleach.

- Bleach concentrations can vary between 5% and 6%.

- Quantities given in this table are approximate and are rounded to the nearest practical measurement. Amounts given are calculated in accordance with reaching a chlorine concentration of 100 mg/L

Key:

tbsp: tablespoon

gal: gallon

1 cup = 8 fluid ounces = 16 tablespoons

1 gallon = 16 cups

Using a 5-gallon bucket, mix the bleach from Table 1 with 3-5 gallons of water (12-19 liters).

Remove the vent cap.

Pour the bleach water mixture into the well using a funnel. Avoid all electrical connections. Attach a clean hose to the nearest hose bib and use it to circulate water back into the well for thorough mixing.

Rinse the inside of the well casing with a garden hose or bucket for 5-10 minutes.

Open all faucets inside the home and run the water until you notice a strong odor of chlorine (bleach) at each faucet. Turn off all faucets and allow the solution to remain in the well and plumbing for a minimum of 12 hours.

After at least 12 hours, attach a hose to an outside faucet and drain the chlorinated water onto a non-vegetated area such as a driveway. Continue draining until the chlorine odor disappears. Avoid draining into open sources of water (streams, ponds, etc.).

Turn on all indoor faucets and run water until the chlorine odor disappears.

Until well water has been tested, boil it (rolling boil for 1 minute) before use or utilize an alternative water source should be used. Wait at least 7-10 days after disinfection, then have the water in your well sampled. Water sampling cannot be done until all traces of chlorine have been flushed from the system.

Sampling/Testing After Disinfection

Wait at least 7 to 10 days to test the water after disinfection to ensure that the chlorine has been thoroughly flushed from the system.

Contact your local health department for water sampling and testing information or contact your state laboratory certification officer to find a certified lab near you. You can also get this number from the U.S. Environmental Protection Agency's Safe Drinking Water Hotline (800-426-4791).

Sample the water for total coliform and either E. coli or fecal coliform bacteria to confirm that the water is safe to drink.

If results show no presence of total coliforms or fecal coliforms, the water can be considered safe to drink from a microbial standpoint.

Follow up with two additional samples, one in the next 2 to 4 weeks and another in 3 to 4 months.

Check the safety of your water over the long term: continue to monitor bacterial quality at least twice per year or more often if you suspect any changes in your water quality.

If results show the presence of any coliform bacteria, repeat the well disinfection process and resample. If tests continue to show the presence of bacteria, contact your local health department for assistance.

13. CONCLUSION

You have just been exposed to just about everything you could ever need to know about water and how to keep your family safely hydrated during emergency situations.

You learned about:

- diseases that you can catch from drinking unclean water and how they can harm you.

- other toxins and contaminants that you might find in a water supply.

- the ways you can test your water sources for safety.

- the adverse effects of not getting staying properly hydrated.

- building a long term water storage plan for your and your family.

- the various ways you can clean suspected dirty water so that it is safe to drink.

- the myriad ways you can find alternative water sources in emergency situations.

- and much more...

Now it is time to start applying all this knowledge to your particular situation and become water secure.

To avoid paralysis of analysis, take small actions first. Take an easy action first so you get the satisfaction that comes from moving forward on a plan. Go out right now and build up a few week emergency water stash.

Then work to make your storage program more robust. Research and purchase a water treatment system that is right for you. Or look at large storage containers that could work in your home. Or start planting a water garden. Build on your program day by day and you will soon have a bulletproof water program that will keep your family safe and healthy through any emergency.

And here is a final bit of advise... The internet is your friend. Use it to further explore any of the topics in this book and expand your knowledge on the topics discussed here.

The internet is a great source of illustrated how to's and guides which will give you a deeper understanding of everything discussed in this book. When you find tutorials that are useful to you, print them out and keep them in a preparedness folder for reference when you need them.

If you are not sure where to start, just go to your favorite search engine and type in relevant search terms to find what you need. You will be pleasantly amazed at the volume of useful how to's that you will find.

And be sure to peruse the appendices. They are full of suggested products, web resources and much more.

APPENDIX 1: COMMERCIAL SUPPLIES

There are many products that come in handy when building up your water reserves. While not comprehensive, the product described below make a good starting point for your research.

Note: *We often reference a specific product name from a manufacturer. These product names can change from time to time so if you find a particular product is discontinued, just check with the manufacturer to see what is their most recent version of the product.*

Water Filtration Systems

There are many water filtration systems. For purposes of this list, we are only looking at systems you might use for every day use and/or survival purposes. We are not looking at whole house systems.

Countertop water filters - There are many water filter systems that sit on your countertop. You pour water into the upper chamber and clean water drips into the lower tank. Common brands include Brita, Pur, Aquasana and ZeroWater.

Emergency water filters – These filters are made for emergency situations. Major brands include LifeStraw, Big Berkey, SteriPEN, Katadyn andAquamira.

Water Chemicals

There are a variety of chemicals you can stockpile to treat your water supplies. Some are for purification and others are to allow the water to be stored long term.

- Basic liquid chlorine – Pure chlorine like Clorox is a fundamental water purification chemical.

- Liquid iodine – There are a variety of brands like Lugols iodine solution that do a great job.

- Water purification tablets – These are great because they are small, easy to carry and have a long life. Some brands include Portable Aqua, Aquamira, MSR Aquatabs, Katadyn Micropur Purification Tablets and Rothco Military Water Purification Powder Packets. There are others but this will give you a good starting point.

- Long term water stabilizer – When you store water for more than six months, you want to stabilize it. Stabilizers keep the water potable for several years. We recommend 7C's Water Preserver.

Water Storage Systems

There are a huge variety of water storage systems available. We will discuss a few but this is definitely an area that you need to research to choose the best solution for your situation. There are literally hundreds of suppliers. Just be sure that the system you choose is made with food safe materials and offers easy access to the stored water and you will be fine with any choice you make.

- WaterBOB – The WaterBOB system is an excellent system. It is a collapsible bladder that doesn't take up much space. You place it in your bathtub and fill it. It holds up to 100 gallons – and it includes a pump to remove water as you need it. This product is highly recommended – especially in areas where you have advance warning of a potential disaster.

- WaterBrick – WaterBricks are an amazing water storage container and system. They are designed to be safely stackable up to four feet high – making them a very space effective water storage system. Full sized bricks hold 3.5 gallons and half bricks contain ½ that amount. This makes them very easy to work with by anyone in your household.

- SureWater Tanks – These water safe tanks come in two sizes from 260 gallons and 525 gallons. They are designed to allow easy filling and extraction of water and are an excellent large storage option. You can find them at http://www.surewatertanks.com/.

- Poly- Mart – This company (https://poly-mart.com/products/)makes a variety of emergency water containers in sizes ranging from 100 to 500 gallons. They also make a variety of rainwater capture systems and massive water storage tanks up to 5,000 gallons in size.

Water Testing Kits

Being able to trust your primary water source on a day to day basis is vitally important to your health. As events in Flint, MI have proven, your best source of trusted information related to your health is you.

Home water testing kits are pretty robust and relatively cheap – allowing just about anyone to test their water source at least once a year to be sure it is safe. Most give instant results. One requires the sample to be sent to a lab for processing – but it is much more comprehensive than what you can do with instant test kits.

Here are several kits that will help you ensure your water supply is safe.

- First Alert WT1 Drinking Water Test Kit – This kit tests bacteria, lead, pesticides, nitrates/nitrites, chlorine, hardness and pH. The kit tests to EPA standards.

- HM Digital TDS-EZ Water Quality TDS Tester – This tester is an inexpensive digital tool that instantly check your overall water quality. It measures the total dissolved solids (TDS) in the water including salts, metals and minerals. The lower the TDS level, the purer the water, with 0 ppm being pure H2O. Note: This test meter only tests inorganics. It does not test biological contaminants.

- Watersafe WS425W Well Water Test Kit – Designed to test the quality of your well water, the WS425W is a fast, easy-to-use water test kit designed to detect hazardous contaminants in municipal and private well drinking water. The kit can detect the presence of bacteria, pesticides, lead, nitrate, nitrite, total chlorine level, pH, iron, copper and hardness.

• Digital Aid Water Quality Test Meter – is another meter testing for total dissolved solids. It has the same essential function as the HM Digital meter listed previously.

• EnviroTestKits – This test kit hugely comprehensive, performing 150 different quality tests. You do need to send it their lab for processing but if you are looking for a full spectrum test kit, this is the one you want. It tests your drinking water for a minimum of 150 Contaminants including a variety of bacteria, 31 different metal contaminants, inorganic compounds, pesticides and much more.

• Test Assured Drinking Water Test Kit – This kit tests for a variety of contaminants. In 10 minutes, you will have test results on the following contaminants: lead, pesticides, bacteria/coliform, iron, nitrates, nitrites, chlorine level, copper, alkalinity, pH and water hardness.

• PurTest Home Drinking Water Analysis Test Kit – This kit tests for 11 contaminants including: bacteria, lead, pesticide, iron, alkalinity, pH, hardness, chlorine, copper, nitrate & nitrite.

• Watts Premier 173006 All-In-One Water Test Kit – This kit tests for a variety of contaminants and delivers results in minutes. It tests for: free chlirine, total chlorine, chloride, pH, alkalinity, total hardness, nitrate, nitrite, iron, sulfate, hydrogen sulfate, copper, lead, pesticide and bacterial contamination.

- Pro-Lab WQ105 Water Quality Do It Yourself Test Kit - This kit tests your water for pH (acidity), total alkalinity, total chloride, total hardness, hydrogen sulfide, iron, copper, nitrates, nitrites, iron and bacteria.

- PurTest Bacteria Water Test Kit — The PurTest water kit tests for three categories of contaminants. It tests for E. coli and coliform bacteria, nitrates and nitrites.

Water Gathering Systems – well pumps, etc.

Hand powered well pumps and similar systems are great to have on hand if you have a well on your property. Some brands to consider include Lehman's Well Bucket, EarthStraw Code Red Pump, the Storm Pump, Bison Pumps and for a powered solution, consider solar pumps from http://www.simplepump.com.

APPENDIX 2: MASTER WATER SUPPLY LIST

This list represents many items you would want to include in your emergency water supply to help you gather, save and conserve water. This list is over and above the actual water that you have stored. It is not meant to be a comprehensive list. Depending on your situation, I'm sure you can think of other things you would add to your list – or things that would not benefit you. As always, preparedness decisions must be made based on your particular situation and circumstances.

- Five gallon buckets for sanitation purposes. These can be used for washing clothes or for "garbage bag" toilets as well as many other sanitation related uses.

- Five gallon food safe buckets with covers to allow you to gather water from a variety of natural sources: rain, streams, ponds, etc.

- Various empty water storage containers. These will be used to store any treated water from nature or for additional water when your normal sully is active for a short time. These can be one gallon or five gallon in size.

- A supply of baby wipes for general water free body cleanliness issues.

- Liquid chlorine or chlorine tablets like the Portable Aqua brand to sanitize natural water sources.

- Clothes drying racks to dry your clothes after hand washing them.

- Tools to dig ditches to dispose of waste so it doesn't accumulate in your house. You may also include several garbage cans for waste storage that will later be transferred off site.

- Electrolyte drink, powder or the raw ingredients to make your own electrolyte mix.

- A good gravity filtration system to quickly filter large quantities of water. Systems like the Big Berkey can treat many gallons of water very quickly.

- Clean cotton cloth to use as a prefilter to remove large particles from dirty water sources before filtering it through your water treatment system. This prefiltering extends the life of your system's filter.

- Hand sanitizer to keep your hands clean.

- Lawn and leaf bags and other sizes of very heavy duty

garbage bags to help control waste disposal.

- Iodine tablets for purifying water.

- Water distillation system that doesn't require electricity to work.

- Water testing kits.

- Cleaning supplies for laundry, dishes, etc. Try to find products that are easy to wash out as you will not want to use gallons of water to wash the cleaning supplies out of the clothes, off the dishes, etc.

APPENDIX 3: WATER SOURCES BY ENVIRONMENT

This appendix looks at various extreme environments and lists the water sources you are likely to have available if you find yourself in such an environment during an emergency.

Frigid areas

Frigid areas include anywhere where a cold enough winter has set in that the only sources of water available are snow and ice.

If you are in this environment, there are a few things to be aware of.

1. Always melt the solid water into liquid first. Eating snow directly and ice can lower body temperature and lead to dehydration.

2. The show and ice are only as clean as the environment

where they are found. That means that there could be contaminants in ice and in snow – especially if it has been sitting on the ground for a period of time.

3. Sea ice is likely to be salty. Don't drink it if it tastes salty.

The Sea/Beach

If you are stranded at sea or at the beach, getting potable water is difficult without having equipment. Your only sources are capturing rain water and removing salt from the salt water with a desalter kit or by a distillation process.

Desert

The desert is another tough environment but there are quite a few places that have water if you know where to look.

Desert water sources include:

- At low, shaded areas of ground. This includes low areas in valleys, under low spots of dry river beds, at the foot of cliffs or rock outcrops and anywhere where you find green plants growing.

- Cactus

- Depressions or holes in rocks can contain water

- Condensation on metal caused by the extreme temperature changes from night to day

- Animal trails

- Flocks of birds gathered in an area

Jungle

Jungles are by their very nature wet. The biggest problem in a jungle is finding clean water sources. If you have water purification equipment – like a LifeStraw – you will be able to make use of many easy to find water sources.

But if not, generally safe water sources include:

- Water vines

- Roots of trees

- Palm trees

- Banana plants

- Vegetation still

- Solar still

Captured rainwater may or may not be clean. If it falls through the trees, it could pick up lots of contaminants on the trees as it falls to the ground.

APPENDIX 4: ADDITIONAL RESOURCES

Here are several government web resources related to water, water safety and storage.

- https://www.ready.gov/water – good resource on water needs during an emergency. It also includes links related to other preparedness topics.

- http://www.cdc.gov/safewater/storage.html - Good overview of safe water storage containers useful for emergency situations as well as a discussion of what makes a safe water container.

- http://www.cdc.gov/healthywater/emergency/drinking/emergency-water-supply-preparation.html – CDC site discussing various issues about safe water in an emergency.

- https://www.fema.gov/pdf/library/f&web.pdf – A pdf file from FEMA on food and water in emergency situations/

- http://emergency.cdc.gov/preparedness/kit/water/ - CDC document on building a water kit.

- http://www.deq.utah.gov/Topics/emergencies/drinkingwater/emergencywaterstorage.htm – Great document from the Utah state government on water storage and emergency disinfection in an emergency.

- http://www.doh.wa.gov/Emergencies/EmergencyPreparednessandResponse/Factsheets/WaterPurification – is a document from Washington state on how to purify water.

- http://www.wikihow.com/Make-a-Water-Still – instructions on how to make a water still

- http://www.wikihow.com/Make-a-Water-Filter – instructions on how to build a homemade water filter

- https://extension.usu.edu/waterquality/files-ou/Publications/Homemade-water-purifier.pdf is a pdf detailing how to make a homemade water purifier

- http://www.wikihow.com/Build-a-Rainwater-Collection-System – instructions on how to build a rainwater collection system.

- http://www.wikihow.com/Dig-a-Well – great look at how a well is drilled.

- http://www.wikihow.com/Make-an-Outhouse – how to build an outhouse.

- https://en.wikipedia.org/wiki/Composting_toilet – everything you need to know about composting toilets

- http://www.motherearthnews.com/diy/home/how-to-make-a-solar-still-ze0z1209zsch.aspx – discusses how to make a really nice solar still complete with a pdf document with the assembly instructions.

- http://www.wikihow.com/Make-Water-in-the-Desert – a few examples of vegetation based stills

- http://www.cdc.gov/diseasesconditions/ - A-Z list of diseases giving more details on all the diseases discussed in this book plus many others.

- http://www.cdc.gov/healthywater/drinking/public/water_diseases.html – a quick link point for water related diseases in the CDC A-Z index.

- https://en.wikipedia.org/wiki/Dehydration – a great resource for additional details on dehydration.

- https://www.epa.gov/ccl/types-drinking-water-contaminants – an EPA article on contaminants you might find in your drinking water.

- http://www.cdc.gov/healthywater/drinking/public/water_treatment.html – great illustration of how water treatment works in public water supplies.

- https://www.epa.gov/sites/production/files/2015-11/documents/2005_09_14_faq_fs_homewatertesting.pdf – EPA home water testing FAQ pdf document.

APPENDIX 5: WHERE TO STORE WATER IN YOUR HOUSE

Water takes up a lot of space so it is sometimes necessary to get creative in finding places to store enough water for your family in an emergency. With good planning and proper storage container selection, you will find a wide variety of places to store your water.

But there are some rules you will want to follow. It is generally best to store your water in a cool, dark place. It is not advisable to store in someplace that gets hot or freezes. So a garage, attic or storage shed is not an ideal place to store water.

That said, let's take a look at all the places you can store water in your house.

Basement

If your house has a basement, it might be a good storage

location for your water supply – especially large storage tanks.

It generally stays cool all year around – especially if the basement is partially or completely underground. And it usually has room (or can be made to have room) to set up one or more large tanks.

Since you probably store other things in your basement, just be sure to keep your water supply away from any hazardous chemicals that you may have stored there.

The basement does have one drawback however. You will need to haul water up a flight of stair. This can be anywhere from inconvenient to quite difficult depending on your physical condition.

Under the stairs

If you have a two story house, you have a large storage space under the stairs. It might currently be closed off but with a little bit of carpentry, it can be made accessible.

If you access this space, it can be lined with shelves or just used as free for all storage and it is a great place to store water – especially if you are using stackable containers. It is probably convenient to your kitchen so it is convenient to access the water and it is reasonably temperature controlled as it is in your living space.

Closets

Closets are another great place to store food. Since they are usually of a consistent height, it is pretty easy to install shelves – much easier than under the stairs. Or you can just lay flat water storage containers on the floor and put a board over the top of them and not lose much space in your closet at all.

Extra room in the main living space

It may be that you have an extra room in your house where you can stack water bottles against a wall without impacting your day to day living situation.

There are even people who get creative with stackable water bottles and use them to build furniture. Make a nice stack and put a glass top on it and you have a nice coffee table or end table. Or two stacks with a flat door put on top can make for a pretty decent desk. You get the idea. By incorporating the water storage bottles into your living situation, you can find many places to store water that is 100% out of the way yet very convenient to reach.

Under the bed

One place that most people overlook is under the bed. For many of us, this is an unused storage space – just collecting lint balls or the stray sock. It can be used for water storage. Just use storage containers that fit under the bed.

I'm sure that if you look around your house, you can find lots more "dead" spaces that can be used to store your prepping water supplies. Just remember that water should be rotated on a six month basis unless it has been treated with a water preserver – or is store bought with an expiration date a few years in the future. So keep rotation things in mind when storing it. If it is too difficult to get to, you will not rotate it and the water may need treatment at the time you need it the most.

ABOUT THE AUTHOR

Steven Chabotte has been fascinated by the concept of being able to live off the land his whole life. Much of his childhood was invested in exploring the woods around his family home, learning about the edible plants nearby, local animals, woodcraft skills and much more.

He became serious about the idea of prepping in 1992 when he was living only 50 miles away from the center of Hurricane Andrew which totally wiped out Homestead Florida and caused damage even his neighborhood.

Now he practices practical prepping – ensuring that his home and family is ready for any likely disaster that may be thrown at him – whether it be an eight hour power outage like he had two days before writing this sentence or a disaster lasting for months.

To learn more about all aspects of prepping, be sure to visit his website The Weekend Prepper at http://www.TheWeekendPrepper.com and to subscribe to prepper tips, his weekly newsletter keeping you up to date on all issues relating to your comfortable survival during emergency situations.

NOW IT IS TIME TO TAKE ACTION . . .

Now that you've completed this book, take some action on your water storage plan.

- Clean some space in your house to store water.
- Buy some extra drinking water and start a rotation system to keep it fresh
- Start researching water treatment chemicals and supplies
- Check out local natural water resources

Just do something every day that makes you and your family more secure for any potential future emergency. You will be amazed how quickly you can become water secure by just taking little steps every day.

Give a review:

If you found this book helpful for your prepping activities, help spread the word by adding a review of it on Amazon. Reviews on Amazon let give other's insight into the content of a book and help them make a more informed purchase decision. Consider a review as a way of paying good karma forward.

Stay in touch with The Weekend Prepper:

Website: http://www.theweekendprepper.com

Facebook:
https://www.facebook.com/TheWeekendPrepper

Twitter: https://twitter.com/WeekendPrepper

INDEX

Made in the USA
Las Vegas, NV
27 September 2021

31154923R00125